SANS DÉTOUR

A complete reference manual for French Grammar

Priscilla Gac-Artigas

Monmouth University

Gustavo Gac-Artigas

Prentice Hall, Upper Saddle River, NJ 07458

Library of Congress Cataloging-in-Publication Data
Gac-Artigas, Priscilla.
        Sans détour: a complete reference manual for French grammar / Priscilla and Gustavo
Gac-Artigas.
        p. cm.
        ISBN 0-13-022055-8
1. French language -- Grammar -- Handbooks, manuals, etc.
I. Gac-Artigas, Gustavo, 11/08/99   II. Title/
PC2112.G27   2000
448.2'421--dc21

                                        99-047376

*To Melina and Alejandro Gac-Artigas,
who granted us part of the precious time
of their childhood to complete this book.*

Editor in Chief: Rosemary Bradley
Development Editor: Mariam Pérez-Roch Rohlfing
Executive Managing Editor: Ann Marie McCarthy
Project Manager: Elizabeth Dice
Interior Design: Hispanex, Inc.
Cover Design: Bruce Kenselaar
Buyer: Tricia Kenny
Executive Marketing Manager: Ilse Wolfe

This book was set in 11/13 Sabon by Hispanex, Inc.,
and was printed and bound by Courier Companies, Inc.
The cover was printed by Phoenix Color Corp.

First and second editions previously
published by To the Point Books.

Printed in the United States of America
10 9 8 7 6 5 4 3 2 1

ISBN 0-13-022055-8

PRENTICE-HALL INTERNATIONAL (UK) LIMITED, *London*
PRENTICE-HALL OF AUSTRALIA PTY. LIMITED, *Sydney*
PRENTICE-HALL CANADA INC., *Toronto*
PRENTICE-HALL HISPANOAMERICANA, S.A., *Mexico*
PRENTICE-HALL OF INDIA PRIVATE LIMITED, *New Delhi*
PRENTICE-HALL OF JAPAN, INC., *Tokyo*
PEARSON EDUCATION ASIA PTE. LTD., *Singapore*
EDITORA PRENTICE-HALL DO BRASIL, LTDA., *Rio de Janeiro*

CONTENTS

PREFACE

Sans Détour is an indispensable, complete, student-friendly and self-teaching grammar reference book for beginners as well as advanced students of French. Concise, accurate and informative descriptions cover all the complexity of specific grammatical points, thus saving a large amount of time for students who are writing papers or reviewing for tests. The conceptual economy of the charts and formulas included in **Sans Détour** assures mastery in the clearest, fastest, and most effortless way possible.

Beyond the classroom, **Sans Détour** provides a lifelong reference guide for anybody eager to learn the French language.

ACKNOWLEDGMENTS

We would like to thank
Rosemary Bradley, Editor in Chief, and Mariam Rohlfing, our Editor.
Thanks for your wise suggestions and your understanding of our purpose; for your smiles and graciousness. It has been a pleasure working with both of you.

We would also like to thank our colleagues at universities across the country for their helpful comments and suggestions regarding **Sans Détour**. Among these, we especially thank: Edwige Gamache, *Northern Michigan University*; MaryJo Cleins, *Molloy College*; Michael Danahy, *University of Mississippi*; and Chana Newman, *Point Park College*.

ABOUT THE AUTHORS

Dr. Priscilla Gac-Artigas teaches Spanish and French at Monmouth University, New Jersey, USA. In the pedagogical field she co-authored with Gustavo Gac-Artigas: **Sans Détour**, for French; **Directo al Grano**, for Spanish and **To the Point**, for English. She is the editor of the Web site *Reflexiones: Essays on Contemporary Spanish-American Women Writers* (http:www.monmouth.edu/~pgacarti/index.html)

Dr. Gac-Artigas has been distinguished with the Elena Ralle-1994 Prize awarded by the University of Franche-Comté for "the research that best contributes to the knowledge and diffusion of Latin American culture."

Gustavo Gac-Artigas, Chilean writer and theater director, is author of *El solar de Ado, Tiempo de soñar, ¡E il orbo era rondo!, Dalibá la brujita del Caribe, Ex-Iliadas, Un asesinato corriente,* and *Seis historias Carrolltonesas.*

Mr. Gac-Artigas has been distinguished with the Poetry Park Prize in the Netherlands, and as one of the Cecil and Ida Green Honors Professors by Texas Christian University, and has received critical acclaim for his writing.

CHAPTER 1

Articles

Articles are words used to signal nouns and specify their application.

✔ Articles are **definite** or **indefinite**.

✔ Articles are either masculine or feminine, singular or plural, according to the gender and number of the noun with which they are used.

✔ All nouns have gender in French.

1-1 Definite articles *refer to specific members of a group or class.*

before a consonant			before a vowel or a mute *h*		
	masculine	feminine		masculine	feminine
singular	le	la	singular	l'	l'
plural	les	les	plural	les	les

*le does not contract in front of the numbers **un, huit,** or **onze.**

le huit janvier

*le and la do not contract in front of an aspirate **h: la** honte, **la** haine, **le** héros, **la** hauteur, **le** haricot, **le** hasard

✔ The definite articles **le, la, l', les** are equivalent to *the.*

1-1a Contractions with à

✔ The articles **le** and **les** contract with the preposition **à,** meaning: *to, in,* or *at.*

à + le → au à + les → aux

Je vais **au** théâtre. Je parle **aux** étudiants.
I go to the theater. *I speak to the students.*

✔ The forms **l'** and **la** do not contract with **à.**

à + l' . . . → à l' . . . à + la → à la

J'étudie à l'université. Je vais à la bibliothèque.
I study at the university. *I go to the library.*

Contractions with *à*

| | before a consonant | | | before a vowel or a mute *h* | |
	masculine	feminine		masculine	feminine
singular	au	à la	singular	à l'...	à l'...
plural	aux	aux	plural	aux	aux

1-1b Contractions with *de*

✔ Le and les also contract with the preposition **de**, meaning *from*, *about*, *of*, or *some*.

de + le → du

Je parle **du** dernier roman de Marguerite Duras.
I am talking about Marguerite Duras' last novel.

de + les → des

Je parle **des** romans de Marguerite Duras.
I am talking about Marguerite Duras' novels.

✔ The definite articles **l'** and **la** do not contract with **de**.

de + l'... → de l'...

Je parle **de l'**oeuvre de Marcel Proust.
I am talking about Marcel Proust's creative work.

de + la → de la

Je parle **de la** poésie de Rimbaud.
I am talking about Rimbaud's poetry.

Contractions with *de*

| | before a consonant | | | before a vowel or a mute *h* | |
	masculine	feminine		masculine	feminine
singular	du	de la	singular	de l'	de l'
plural	des	des	plural	des	des

1-1c Uses and omissions

Use of definite articles

✔ When the noun designates a person or an object that is specific, use a definite article.

La Bastille était une prison.
The Bastille was a prison.

Le soleil n'est pas une planète.
The sun is not a planet.

✔ Use definite articles to refer to a noun in an ample or generic sense.

Les voitures Renault roulent bien.
The Renault cars run well.

Le lait est bon pour la santé.
Milk is good for your health.

✔ With nouns representing a broad category, group, or profession, use a definite article.

Les écrivains doivent sauvegarder les rêves de l'humanité.
Writers should protect the dreams of humanity.

✔ Use definite articles to make generalizations or to refer to abstract concepts.

Il faut conquérir **la** liberté
Freedom must be conquered.

✔ In front of the days of the week, use **le** to indicate that an action is habitually done that day.

Le mardi je fais les courses.
I buy groceries every Tuesday.

✔ Use a definite article to contrast two different days or dates.

Elle est venue me voir **le** vendredi et elle est repartie **le** dimanche.
She came to see me on Friday, and left on Sunday.

✘ However, to refer to a specific day or to indicate an occurrence which takes place only once, the article is omitted.

Mardi prochain je partirai pour la France.
Next Tuesday I will leave for France.

✔ Use a definite article in front of a date.

Son anniversaire est **le** 6 mars.
His/Her birthday is on March 6.

✔ Definite articles are used with the seasons.

C'est **l'**hiver; il neige.
It's winter; it is snowing.

✔ Use definite articles in front of holidays.

le jour de l'an
New Year's day

La Toussaint
All Saints' Day

le 14 juillet
July the fourteenth

exceptions: Noël
Christmas

Pâques
Easter

✘ *But* a definite article is not used before the names of months.

La rentrée est au mois de septembre.
School begins in September.

✔ Use definite articles after the following verbs to express preference, likes or dislikes.

adorer	aimer	préférer	détester	apprécier

J'adore **les** voyages.
I love to travel.

J'aime **la** bonne table.
I love to eat well.

Je n'aime pas **la** bière, je préfère **le** vin.
I don't like beer, I prefer wine.

Ils détestent **le** fromage.
They hate cheese.

✔ Definite articles are used to designate a specific object.

Donnez-moi **le** livre de français, s'il vous plaît.
Hand me the French book, please.

✔ Use definite articles with names of substances, materials, and processes.

Le pétrole est le résultat de **la** transformation du matériel organique.
Oil is the result of the transformation of organic material.

✔ Definite articles appear before titles.

le Président
the President

la reine
the Queen

le Premier ministre
the Prime Minister

✔ Before names modified by an adjective, use a definite article.

C'est mon ami **le** vieux François.
It is my friend, old François.

✗ However a definite article is not used when addressing a person directly or preceding **monsieur**, **madame**, or **mademoiselle**.

Bonjour, docteur Martin!
Good morning, Doctor Martin!

Bonsoir, mademoiselle Duval!
Good evening, Miss Duval!

✔ Use **les** with family names, but do not make the name plural.

Les Duponts sont en vacances.
The Duponts are on vacation.

✔ Use definite articles before the name of languages, except after the preposition **en**.

L'italien est la langue de l'opéra, **le** français la langue de l'amour et **l'**anglais la langue du commerce.
Italian is the language of opera; French is the language of love, and English is the language of business.

Gustavo écrit **en** espagnol, la langue du réalisme merveilleux.
Gustavo writes in Spanish, the language of magical realism.

✔ After the verb **parler,** the definite article can be omitted when the name of the language immediately follows the verb.

Je voudrais parler français couramment.   Je ne parle pas (le) portugais.
I would like to speak French fluently.   *I don't speak Portuguese.*

Vous parlez anglais, mais vous parlez aussi très bien le français.
You speak English, but you also speak French very well.

✔ Use definite articles before nouns used to identify national or local origin.

les Américains   **les** Parisiens
Americans   *Parisians*

✔ Use a definite article before the first noun in a compound-noun construction.

la classe de français   **le** chef de famille   **le** maître d'hôtel
the French class   *the head of the family*   *the head waiter*

✔ Definite articles are used in front of fields of study.

J'étudie **les** mathématiques, **la** physique et **la** biologie.
I study math, physics, and biology.

✔ With parts of the body and clothing, use a definite article with a reflexive verb. However, if the verb is not reflexive, the possessive adjective is used.

Elle se lave **les** mains.   Elle se coiffe les cheveux.
She washes her hands.   *She brushes her hair.*

Elle lave **ses** (petites) mains.   Elle coiffe ses cheveux.
She washes her small hands.   *She brushes her hair.*

✔ Use a definite article with expressions of rates and prices.

Les fraises coûtent dix francs **le** kilo.
Strawberries cost ten francs a kilo.

✔ Use definite articles to form the superlative.

Daliba, la petite sorcière des Caraïbes c'est son roman **le plus** poétique.
Daliba, la petite sorcière des Caraïbes is his most poetic novel.

C'est son amie **la plus** fidèle.
She is his most faithful friend.

✔ Use definite articles with geographic names: continents, countries, provinces, regions, oceans, rivers, mountains. States follow the rules of countries.

La France et l'Espagne sont des pays voisins.
France and Spain are neighboring countries.

La Seine traverse Paris.
The Seine runs through Paris.

Je connais bien **la** Georgie et **le** Texas.
I know Georgia and Texas well.

✔ Use definite articles with the names of colors.

Le vert est ma couleur préférée.
Green is my favorite color.

1-1d Omissions:

✘ Omit the indefinite article after the preposition **de** when introducing the name of an unmodified feminine place.

Vous venez **de** France?
Do you come from France?

✘ In front of the names of cities or after **en** used with feminine place names, the definite article is omitted.

J'aime visiter **Avignon** quand je vais **en** France.
I like to visit Avignon when I go to France.

Exceptions are: **Le** Havre, **Le** Mans, **La** Haye, **Le** Caire, **La** Havane.

✔ However, when the name of the city is modified, the article is used.

Paris est merveilleux.
Paris is wonderful.

Le <u>vieux</u> Paris est merveilleux.
The old Paris is wonderful.

✘ The article is omitted when a noun denoting a profession, political belief, religion, or nationality follows **être**.

Il **est** médecin.
He is a doctor.

John **est** américain.
John is American.

Elle **est** démocrate.
She is a democrat.

✘ Omit the article before each noun in a series.

Tout est à vendre: livres, cahiers, crayons, et stylos.
Everything is for sale: books, notebooks, pencils, and pens.

✘ Omit the definite article after the preposition **en**.

Elle part **en** vacances.
She is going on vacation.

Il est fort **en** math.
He is good at math.

✔ However, definite articles are used in some idiomatic expressions.

en l'absence de	en l'air	en l'an de	en l'honneur de
in the absence of	*in the air*	*in the year of*	*in homage to*

1-2 Indefinite articles *refer to any unspecified member of a general group or class.*

✔ The singular forms correspond to **a** and **an** and the plural forms to **some** or **a few.** In some cases they correspond to **about** or **around.**

✔ Indefinite articles must agree in number and gender with the noun they modify.

	masculine	feminine	
singular	**un**	**une**	*a/an*
plural	**des**	**des**	*some, a few, about*

un étudiant → des étudiants
une étudiante → des étudiantes
a student   some students

1-2a   Uses and omissions

✔ Indefinite articles precede count nouns.

une banane → des bananes
a banana   some bananas
un livre → des livres
a book   some books

✔ In negative sentences **des** changes to **de** or **d'** before the direct object, except **être**, after **un** meaning *only one,* or when there are two opposing nouns.

Tu as **un** chien?   Non, je n'ai pas **de** chien.
Do you have a dog?   *No, I don't have a dog.*

C'est **un** chien?   Non, ce n'est pas **un** chien, c'est **un** unicorne.
Is it a dog?   *No, it is not a dog, it is a unicorn.*

Pierre n'a pas dit **un** mot.   Je ne veux pas **de** sandwich, je voudrais **une** quiche.
Pierre didn't say a word.   *I don't want a sandwich, I would like a quiche.*

✘ The indefinite article **des** is omitted after expressions of quantity.

beaucoup de	trop de	une foule de	un tas de
much/many	*too much/many*	*a lot of*	*a pile of*
assez de	combien de	autant de	tant de
enough	*how much*	*as much/many*	*so much/many*
peu de	un peu de	plus de	moins de
few, little	*a little of*	*more*	*less, fewer.*

Très peu **d**'huîtres ont une perle.
Very few oysters contain a pearl.

Exceptions are: **bien des (du, de la), la moitié des (du, de la), la plupart des (du, de la), encore des (du, de la), le plus grand nombre des (du, de la)**

✗ Indefinite articles are omitted when a noun denoting a profession, political belief, religion, or nationality follows **être**.

Je suis américaine.   Il est étudiant.
I am Americain.   *He is a student.*

✔ *But* the indefinite article is used when the noun that follows **être** is modified by an adjective.

Marilyn est une belle femme.   Victor Hugo est **un** poète romantique.
Marilyn is a beautiful woman.   *Victor Hugo is a romantic poet.*

✔ The indefinite article **de/d'** is used instead of **des** with a plural adjective that precedes a noun.

Nous sommes **de** bons étudiants.
We are good students.

✔ Indefinite articles are used to answer the following question.

Qu'est-ce que c'est?
What is that?

✔ Use the pattern **c'est** . . . c'est un/e (*it/he/she...is*) or **ce sont** (*they are*) for the plural.

C'est un avocat.   **C'est une** étudiante.
He/She is a lawyer.   *She is a student.*

Ce sont des chats.
They are cats.

✔ If Ce (C') is used in place of the pronouns **il(s)** or **elle(s)** when refering to a nationality, political belief, religion, or profession; the indefinite article is used. **Ce (C')** is also used with a modified noun.

C'est une belle voiture.   Ce sont de belles voitures.
It's a beautiful car.   *These are beautiful cars.*

Elle est française.   **C'est une** française.
She is French.   *She is French.*

C'est un républicain.   **Ce sont des** professeurs.
He is a Republican.   *They are professors.*

✗ Indefinite articles are omitted in front of **comme, ni... ni,** and after **avec** and **sans,** when used with an abstract noun.

Il travaille **comme** journaliste.
He works as a journalist.

Il regardait le peintre **sans** curiosité, mais plutôt **avec** sympathie.
He looked at the painter without curiosity, rather with sympathy.

"Cela ne me fait **ni** chaud **ni** froid," a dit l'ignorant.
"That leaves me indifferent," said the ignorant.

Elle étudie *Sans Détour* **avec** enthousiasme.
She is enthusiastically studying Sans Détour.

✘ Indefinite articles are also omitted after a noun that is a complement of another noun.

une belle chemise de nuit
a beautiful nightgown

une maison de campagne
a country house

✘ Indefinite articles are omitted before each noun in a series.

Il a acheté beaucoup d'instruments pour son magasin: pianos, violons, guitares, etc
He bought many instruments for his store: pianos, violins, guitars, etc.

1-3 The partitive article *refers to a part of a whole. It is formed by combining* **de** *and the definite article.*

✔ The partitive article corresponds to **some** or **any**.

Je voudrais **des** fraises.
I would like some strawberries.

✔ Use the partitive article to express any indefinite quantity.

Ils boivent **de l'**eau avec le repas.
They drink water with their meal.

	singular	plural
masculine	du/de l'	des
feminine	de la/de l'	des

1-3a Uses and omissions

✔ Use the partitive article before an abstract noun to express an indefinite quantity, and before a concrete noun referring to a quantity that cannot be counted or is part of a whole.

Il a **du** courage.
He is brave.

Elle aime manger **du** fromage.
She likes to eat cheese.

✔ If you mean to refer to only a part of a concept, and not the whole, use the partitive.

Pierre achète **de la** viande.
Pierre is buying some meat.

Jean mange **du** pain.
Jean eats bread.

Je vous apporte **des** fruits.
I am bringing you some fruit.

✔ The partitive becomes **de** or **d'** in the negative, except after **être**.

Pierre n'achète pas **de** viande.
Pierre doesn't buy meat.

Jean ne mange pas **d'**ananas.
Jean doesn't eat pineapples.

Je ne vous apporte pas **de** fruits.
I am not bringing you any fruit.

but Ce n'est pas **de la** viande.
It is not meat.

✔ When used with a plural adjective that precedes a noun, **des** becomes **de**.

Marie et Anne sont **des** filles. → Ce sont **de** belles filles.
Marie and Anne are girls. *They are beautiful girls.*

Il a **des** amis → Il a **de** bons amis.
He has friends. *He has good friends.*

The exception is when the **adjective** and **noun** are considered a compound noun.

des petits pois   **des** petits fours   **des** grands magasins
green peas   *small fancy cakes*   *department stores*

✔ **De** is also used instead of **des** after expressions of quantity.

assez **de** *enough*	beaucoup **de** *many, a lot of*	trop **de** *too much/many*	tant **de** *so much/many*
peu **de** *little, few*	plus **de** *more*	moins **de** *less, fewer*	un verre **de** *a glass of*
une bouteille **de** *a bottle of*	un kilo **de** *a kilo of*	une douzaine **de** *a dozen of*	un morceau **de** *a piece of*
un mètre **de** *a meter of*	une tranche **de** *a slice of*	une tasse **de** *a cup of*	autant **de** *as much, as many*
combien **de** *how many, how much*		davantage **de** *more*	

Je voudrais une douzaine **d'**oeufs, une tranche **de** jambon, un kilo **de** raisins et une bouteille **de** rouge, s'il vous plaît.
I would like a dozen eggs, a slice of ham, a kilo of grapes, and a bottle of red wine, please.

The exceptions are **bien du, bien de la, bien des**; *many, much, most.*

la plupart des gens   la plupart du temps   encore du thé
most people   *most of the time*   *some more tea*

encore de l'eau   encore des problèmes   encore de la limonade
some more water   *some more difficulties*   *some more lemonade*

Bien des lycéens etudient le français.
Many high schoolers study French.

✗ The adverbs of quantity, **plusieurs** and **quelques,** do not require the partitive.

J'ai mangé **beaucoup de** fruits.
I ate a lot of fruit.

J'ai mangé **quelques** raisins et **plusieurs** fraises.
I ate some grapes and several strawberries.

✗ The partitive is omitted after the preposition **sans.**

Il aime son café **sans** sucre.
He likes his coffee without sugar.

CHAPTER 2

Nouns

Nouns identify the subject of discourse. A noun names persons, places, objects, or ideas.

2-1 Gender of nouns

✔ There are no neuters in French. All nouns are either masculine or feminine.

2-1a Masculine nouns

✔ Names referring to the male of a species are masculine.

> l'homme   le singe   le dinosaure

✔ Names of months, days, seasons, holidays*, cardinal directions, and languages are always masculine.

le premier mai	**le** lundi	**le** printemps
the first of May	*Monday*	*Spring*
le jour de l'an	**le** nord	**le** français
New Year's day	*North*	*French*

*Exceptions are **la Toussaint** and **la Noël**, but if **Noel** is modified by an adjective or in greetings, it is masculine. *Note:* The article is optional with **Noël**.

Elle est venue pour (**la**) Noël.   Je vous souhaite **un Joyeux** Noël.
She came for Christmas.   *I wish you a Merry Christmas.*

✔ Cities are usually masculine except **Marseille, la Nouvelle Orléans,** and **Bruxelles**.

✔ The names of trees and wines are masculine.

un chêne	**un** sapin	**un** Beaujolais	**un** Côte du Rhône
an oak	*a pine*	*a Beaujolais*	*a Côte du Rhône*

✔ Names of colors and metals are masculine.

l'or	l'argent	le cuivre
gold	*silver*	*copper*

Hier j'ai lu *Le rouge et le noir* de Stendhal.
Yesterday I read Le rouge et le noir *by Stendhal.*

✔ Most items of clothing not ending in **e** are masculine.

le soulier	**le** veston
a shoe	*a vest*

✔ Most of the names borrowed from English are masculine.

un parking **le** week-end
le show **un** meeting

2-1b Common masculine endings

-able: câble

-cle: spectacle, miracle, pinacle, siécle, couvercle

-age: recyclage, voyage, décalage, stage, étage, garage, village, visage, patinage, courage, message, fromage, passage, maquillage

-al: journal, récital, animal, cheval, signal, hôpital, local

-ail: travail, éventail, portail

-aire: inventaire, maire, dictionnaire

-eil: soleil, oeil

-asme: enthousiasme, orgasme, fantasme

-at: doctorat, soldat, consulat, chocolat

-eau: bureau, châpeau, oiseau, morceau, gâteau, couteau, bateau, tableau, château, drapeau

-ent: parent, client, président, vent, argent, instrument

-er: danger, banquier, déjeuner, cuisinier, boulanger, épicier, charcutier, dîner

-et: objet, projet, buffet, cabinet

-eur: auteur, chanteur, vendeur, acteur, honneur, bonheur, malheur

-ien: bien, technicien, mécanicien, Canadien, chien

-in: médecin, marin, cousin, voisin, vin

-isme: impérialisme, optimisme, nationalisme, racisme, fascisme, patriotisme

-ment: enseignement, mouvement, gouvernement, monument, bâtiment, établissement

-oir: soir, miroir, couloir, mouchoir, devoir, tiroir, arrosoir

2-1c The following words are exceptions.

-able: la **table**

-age: la p**age**, une im**age**, la c**age**, la pl**age**, la r**age**

-aire: la grammaire

-eau: l'**eau**, la p**eau**

-ent: une d**ent**

-eur: la cand**eur**, la chal**eur**, la froid**eur**, la val**eur**, la p**eur**, la ferv**eur**, la f**leur**

2-1d Feminine nouns

✔ Names referring to the female of a species are feminine.

la femme	**l'**abeille	**la** vache
woman	*bee*	*cow*

✔ Flowers and fruits ending in -e are feminine, while flowers and fruits ending in letters other than -e are masculine.

une marguerite, **une** rose, **un** oeillet, **une** poire, **une** banane, **un** ananas
a daisy, a rose, a carnation, a pear, a banana, a pineapple.

The exception is **une noix,** *a nut.*

✔ Geographic names ending in -e are feminine, except **le** Mexique, **le** Cambodge, et **le** Mozambique, **le** Rhône, and **le** Danube.

✔ All continents ending in -e are feminine.

l'Europe   l'Asie

✔ The names of cars are feminine.

une Citroën   **une** Ford

2-1e Common feminine endings

-ade: cascade, escapade, salade, parade, estrade

-aille: bataille, maille

-aine: Américaine, douzaine

-aison: conjugaison, liaison, terminaison, raison

-ance: confiance, méfiance, enfance, correspondance

-ande: viande, demande, commande

-çon: leçon, façon, rançon

-ée: matinée, journée, entrée, année

-eille: bouteille, vieille, oreille

-ence: patience

-ère: boulangère, épicière

-ette: allumette, alouette, baguette, cigarette, maquette

-esse: caresse, vitesse, paresse, finesse

-eur: chaleur, grandeur, candeur, froideur, valeur, ferveur, fleur

-euse: vendeuse, chanteuse, danseuse

-ie: mélodie, maladie, crémerie, boucherie, épicerie, compagnie, géographie

-sion: expression, télévision, décision, discussion, profession, passion

-té: bonté, liberté, nationalité, vérité

-te: route, croûte, brute

-tié: amitié, pitié

-tion: addition, composition, occupation, exception, question, respiration, formation

-trice: institutrice, actrice, directrice

-tude: attitude, étude, habitude, solitude

-oire: passoire, bouilloire

-que: banque, barque, marque, époque

-ure: verdure, culture, agriculture, voiture

double consonant + e: la ville, la grippe, la sentinelle, la pomme, la classe, la personne, la femme, la richesse

2-1f   Exceptions

-ade: le grade

-çon: le garçon

-ée: le lycée, le musée, le scarabée

-ie: le génie, un incendie, un parapluie

-ion: un camion, un avion

-té: le député, le côté, l'été, le pâté, le traité

-te: le doute

-que: le manque

-ence: le silence

-ette: un squelette

-eur: le bonheur, le malheur

-ure: mercure, murmure

To form the feminine, the ending of some nouns change before adding -e.

CHART 1	NOUNS: MASCULINE → FEMININE	
MASCULINE → FEMININE	MASCULINE → FEMININE	MASCULINE → FEMININE
-er → -ère	-ier → -ière	-et → -ette
-eur → -euse	-ien → -ienne	f → -ve
-on → -onne	-oux → -ouse	teur → -teuse -trice

un boulanger → **une** boulangère   **un** fermier   → **une** fermière
un cadet   → **une** cadette   **un** vendeur   → **une** vendeuse
un chien   → **une** chienne   **un** veuf   → **une** veuve
un patron   → **une** patronne   **un** époux   → **une** épouse
       exception:
       roux   → rousse

un directeur → **une** directrice
un chanteur → **une** chanteuse

2-1g Common nouns with a different form in the feminine

un monsieur	**une** dame	**un** homme	**une** femme
a gentleman	*a lady*	*a man*	*a woman*
le mari	**la** femme	**le** père	**la** mère
the husband	*the wife*	*the father*	*the mother*
le frère	**la** soeur	**le** parrain	**la** marraine
the brother	*the sister*	*the godfather*	*the godmother*
le neveu	**la** nièce	**un** garçon	**une** fille
the nephew	*the niece*	*a boy*	*a girl*
un oncle	**une** tante	**un** roi	**une** reine
an uncle	*an aunt*	*a king*	*a queen*
un mâle	**une** femelle	**un** fils	**une** fille
a male	*a female*	*a son*	*a daughter*

2-1h Some nouns change meaning according to gender.

le mémoire *memo, disssertation*	la mémoire *memory*	le critique *critic*	la critique *criticism*
un aide *assistant*	une aide *help*	le mode *method*	la mode *fashion*
le garde *guard (person)*	la garde *guard (action)*	le poste *job*	la poste *post office*
un livre *book*	une livre *pound*	le tour *turn, tour*	la tour *tower*
le manche *handle*	la manche *sleeve*	le manoeuvre *worker*	la manoeuvre *maneuver*
le voile *veil*	la voile *sail*	le physique *physical self*	la physique *physics*
le mort *dead person*	la mort *death*	le champagne *champagne*	la Champagne *Champagne (province)*
le politique *politician*	la politique *politics*		

2-1i The following are masculine nouns used for both male and female.

un ancêtre	un amateur	un ange	un assassin
un témoin	un bébé	un voyou	un vainqueur

Marie est **un bébé** très mignon.
Marie is a very cute baby.

✔ In general, all nouns referring to professions previously associated with males have remained masculine. However, they may be made feminine by inserting the word **femme** before the noun, or **Madame** before a title. For example, une **femme** médecin (*a female doctor*), **Madame** le Ministre (Madam the Minister).

un agent *an agent*	un auteur *an author*	un chef *a chef*	un compositeur *a composer*
un écrivain *a writer*	un juge *a judge*	un médecin *a doctor*	un ministre *a minister*
un peintre *a painter*	un président *a president*	un professeur *a professor, teacher*	

Simone de Beauvoir est **un** grand **écrivain**.
Simone de Beauvoir is a great writer.

2-1j The following are feminine nouns used for both male and female.

une bête	une brute	une étoile	sa majesté
beast	*brute*	*star*	*her majesty*

une personne	une vedette	une victime
person	*star*	*victim*

Cet enfant est **une victime** de la société.
This child is a victim of society.

Cet homme est **une brute,** il bat sa femme.
This man is a brute; he beats his wife.

2-2 Plural of nouns

✔ The plural of most nouns is formed by adding **-s.**

> •   **singular + s**

une table   des tables
table(s)

✔ Make nouns ending in **-ou** plural by adding **-s.**

> **ou → + s**

un clou   des clous
nail(s)

un trou   des trous
hole(s)

Seven exceptions

bijou → bijoux	caillou → cailloux	chou → choux	
jewel(s)	*stone(s)*	*cabbage*	

genou → genoux	hibou → hiboux	joujou → joujoux	pou → poux
knee(s)	*owl(s)*	*toy(s)*	*louse/lice*

✔ Singular nouns ending in **s, x,** or **z** do not change forms in the plural.

s = s	**x = x**	**z = z**
le fils → les fils	le prix → les prix	le nez → les nez
son(s)	*price(s)*	*nose(s)*

✔ Singular nouns ending in **-au, -eu** and **-eau** form their plural by adding **-x.**

au → + x = aux	**eu → + x = eux**	**eau → + x = eaux**
un tableau → des tableaux	le feu → les feux	eau → eaux
picture(s)	*fire(s)*	*water(s)*

The exception is: un pneu → des pneus
                     tires(s)

✔ Most singular nouns ending in **-al** are pluralized by changing the ending to **-aux**.

al → aux
un chev**al** → des chev**aux**   un journ**al** → des journ**aux**
horse(s)   *newspaper(s)*

The exceptions are:

bal → bals	carnaval → carnavals	festival → festivals
dance(s)	*carnival(s)*	*festival(s)*
final → finals	récital → récitals	régal → régals
finale(s)	*recital(s)*	*treat(s)*

✔ Certain nouns ending in **-ail** become plural by changing **-ail** to **-aux**.

b**ail** → b**aux**	cor**ail** → cor**aux**	ém**ail** → ém**aux**
lease(s)	*coral*	*enamel(s)*
trav**ail** → trav**aux**	vitr**ail** → vitr**aux**	
work(s)	*stained-glass window(s)*	

2-2a   The following nouns have non-standard forms in the plural.

le ciel	les cieux	l'oeil	les yeux
sky	*skies*	*eye*	*eyes*
monsieur	**mes**sieurs	**ma**dame	**mes**dames
mister	*misters*	*madam*	*madams*
mademoiselle	**mes**demoiselles	jeune homme	jeunes gens
miss, young lady	*misses, young ladies*	*young man*	*young people*

Note: **Jeunes gens** refers to a group of young people. Even though the expression refers to men, it can also refer to a group containing both genders. **Jeunes femmes** (*women*), or **jeunes filles** (*girls*) is used for groups that are exclusively female.

CHART 2	NOUNS: SINGULAR → PLURAL		
SINGULAR → + S	S = S	X = X	Z = Z
au → aux	eu → eux	eau → eaux	al → aux

2-2b Some are nouns only used in the plural.

abois *baying*	alentours *environs*	annales *annals*	appointements *salary*	archives *archives*
confins *confines*	décombres *debris*	dépens *costs*	entrailles *entrails*	fiançailles *engagement*
frais *expenses*	funérailles *funeral*	gens *people*	menottes *handcuffs*	moeurs *morals, customs*
pleurs *tears, laments*	pourparlers *discussions*	représailles *reprisals*	ténèbres *darkness*	vacances *vacations*

Il est arrivé aux **confins** de l'univers à la recherche de ses rêves.
He arrived at the confines of the universe in search of his dreams.

2-2c The following nouns have different meanings in the singular and the plural.

singular	plural	singular	plural
affaire *matter, deal, business*	affaires *business, trade, affairs*	bien *well*	biens *property*
frais *cool*	frais *fees/expenses*	reste *remainder*	restes *mortal remains, leftovers*

CHART 3	PLURAL OF COMPOUND NOUNS

verb + noun un **tire**-bouchon *corkscrew*	**noun plural, verb does not change** des **tire**-bouchons *corkscrews*
noun + noun un chou-fleur *cauliflower*	**both plural** des choux-fleurs *cauliflowers*
noun + adjective un coffre-fort *safe box*	**both plural** des coffres-forts *safe boxes*
adjective + noun une longue-vue *telescope*	**both plural** des longues-vues *telescopes*
adjective + adjective un sourd-muet *deaf-mute*	**both plural** des sourds-muets *deaf-mutes*

CHAPTER 3

Adjectives

Adjectives are modifiers that qualify, limit the meaning, or make a noun or pronoun more definite.

✔ Adjectives are classified as descriptive, numerical, possessive, demonstrative, of quantity, and indefinite.

CHART 4	ADJECTIVE PLACEMENT	
PRECEDE	NOUN	FOLLOW
Numerical	N	Descriptive
Descriptive: when used for emphasis or as a poetic device.	O	
Possessive unstressed		Possessive stressed
Demonstrative	U	
Quantitative		
Indefinite	N	

3-1 **Descriptive adjectives** *express a quality of the noun.*

✔ Descriptive adjectives usually follow the noun they qualify, and must agree in gender and number:

Les roses **blanches** sont belles.
White roses are beautiful.

✔ However, when used for emphasis or as a poetic device, descriptive adjectives can precede the noun.

la **blanche** neige qui abrite mes rêves . . .
the white snow that shelters my dreams . . .

✔ The following descriptive adjectives usually precede the noun: **beau, bon, demi, dernier, gentil, grand, gros, jeune, joli, long, mauvais, meilleur, moindre** (numerical), **nouveau, petit, prochain, vieux, vilain**

un **beau** tableau, une **jolie** poupée, un **petit** morceau, un **gros** problème, une **dernière** déception, un **meilleur** avenir
a beautiful picture, a pretty doll, a small piece, a big problem, a last deception, a better future

3-1a Gender

✔ In general, to make an adjective feminine add -**e** to the masculine singular form.

grand → grande	fasciné → fascinée	uni → unie
big, large	*fascinated*	*united*
intelligent → intelligente	émouvant → émouvante	idiot → idiote
intelligent	*touching*	*dumb*
civil → civile	gris → grise	
civil	*gray*	

Some exceptions are:

favori → favorite	sot → sotte	gentil → gentille
favorite	*silly, stupid*	*nice, kind*
bas → basse	gros → grosse	épais → épaisse
low	*fat*	*thick*

✔ Adjectives ending in -**e** don't change.

-e → -e
facile → facile
easy

✔ For adjectives ending in -**el** and -**eil,** add -**le.**

-el → -elle	-eil → -eille
cruel → cruelle	pareil → pareille
cruel	*similar*

✔ Double the consonant and add -**e** to adjectives ending in -**en**, -**et**, and -**on**.

-en → -enne	-et → -ette	-on → -onne
ancien → ancienne	coquet → coquette	bon → bonne
ancient, old	*coquettish*	*good*

For the following exceptions, mark the -e with an **accent grave**, then add -e: **complet, discret, inquiet, secret, concret.**

> -et   →   -ète
> complet   →   complète
> *complete*

✔ Add -e to adjectives ending in **gu.**

> -gu   →   -guë
> ambigue   →   ambiguë
> *ambiguous*
>
> aigu   →   aiguë
> *sharp*   *pointed*

✔ Adjectives ending in **-er** change to **-ère.**

> -er   →   -ère
> fier   →   fière
> *proud*

✔ Adjectives ending in **-eux** and **-eur** change to **-euse.**

> -eux   →   -euse   -eur   →   -euse
> heureux   →   heureuse   moqueur   →   moqueuse
> *happy*   *mocking*

Comparative adjectives are the exception.

antérieur	antérieure	extérieur	extérieure
inférieur	inférieure	intérieur	intérieure
majeur	majeure	meilleur	meilleure
mineur	mineure	postérieur	postérieure
supérieur	supérieure	ultérieur	ultérieure

✔ Most adjectives ending in **-teur** change to **-trice.**

> -teur   →   -trice
> provocateur   →   provocatrice
> *provocative*

✔ Adjectives ending in **-f** change to **-ve.**

> -f   →   -ve
> actif   →   active
> *active*
>
> neuf   →   neuve
> *new*

sportif, agressif, négatif, naïf, imaginatif, impulsif, destructif, attentif, bref, vif

✔ For many adejctives, the -c changes to **che**.

-c   →   -**che**
blanc   →   blan**che**
white

franc   →   fran**che**
frank

Some exceptions are:

grec   →   grecque
greek

public → publique
public

sec   →   sèche
dry

✔ Adjectives retain their masculine form when they follow **c'est, quelqu'un de, quelque chose de, personne de, rien de.**

Mlle. Durand est **quelqu'**un d'important.
Miss Durand is someone very important.

✔ Nouns used as adjectives to describe colors retain their original form.

une chemise crème, un pantalon crème
a beige shirt, a beige pair of pants

une chemise orange, un chapeau orange
an orange shirt, an orange hat

✔ Colors or nouns used as adjectives of color are invariable.

des yeux **noisette**
hazel eyes

The exceptions are écarlate *(scarlet),* **mauve** *(mauve),* **pourpre** *(purple), and* **rose** *(rose-colored).*

une robe **mauve**   des robes **mauves**
a mauve dress   *mauve dresses*

✔ Two adjectives of color used to form a compound adjective are invariable.

des chemises bleu clair ou bleu foncé
light or dark blue shirts

MASCULINE → + E	E = E, É → ÉE	EL → ELLE	EIL → EILLE
en → enne	on → onne	et → tte	gu → guë
er → ère	eux/eur → euse	f → ve	c → che

✔ The adjectives **beau** (*beautiful*), **nouveau** (*new*), **vieux** (*old*), **fou** (*insane*), and **mou** *(soft)* are spelled differently in front of a noun beginning with a vowel or a mute **h,** and have a different feminine form.

Singular

before a consonant masculine	before a vowel or mute *h*	feminine
beau	bel	belle
nouveau	nouvel	nouvelle
vieux	vieil	vieille
fou	fol	folle
mou	mol	molle

Plural

before a consonant, a vowel, or mute *h*	
masculine	feminine
beaux	belles
nouveaux	nouvelles
vieux	vieilles
foux	folles
moux	molles

3-1b Plural of adjectives

✔ In general, adjectives are pluralized by adding **-s** to the singular form.

joli → jolis   intelligente → intelligentes
pretty   *intelligent*

✔ But adjectives ending in **-s** and **-x** do not change.

-s   →   -s   **-x**   →   **-x**
gros   →   gros   heureux   →   heureux
fat   *happy*

✔ Add **-x** to adjectives ending in **-eau**.

-eau   →   **-eaux**
b**eau**   →   b**eaux**
beautiful

nouv**eau**   →   nouv**eaux**
new

✔ Change adjectives ending in **-al** to **-aux**.

-al   →   **-aux**
roy**al**   →   roy**aux**
royal

Exceptions are: banal → banals
                  common

bancal(s)	fatal(s)	final(s)	glacial(s)	natal(s)	naval(s)	tonal(s)
wobbly	*fatal, inevitable*	*final*	*glacial, icy*	*native*	*naval, nautical*	*tonal*

✔ If a single adjective modifies two nouns, one masculine and one feminine, the adjective will take the masculine plural form.

Mon frère et ma soeur sont gentil**s**.
My brother and my sister are kind.

✔ The adjective **demi** does not have a plural form.

✔ **Demi** does not change forms when it precedes a noun.

✔ **Demi** agrees in gender only after a noun showing a complete amount.

une **demi**-heure	un **demi**-kilo	dix kilos et **demi**	dix heures et **demie**
half an hour	*half a kilo*	*ten and a half kilos*	*ten-thirty*

CHART 6	ADJECTIVES SINGULAR → PLURAL	
SINGULAR + S	S = S	X = X
eau → eaux	al → aux	

3-1c Adjectives that change meaning

✔ Some adjectives change their meaning depending on whether they precede (subjective consideration) or follow (objective consideration) the noun.

	precedes	**follows**
ancien	*former*	*old*

C'est l'**ancien** directeur de la troupe.
It's the former director of the troupe.

C'est un théâtre **ancien**.
It's an old theater.

| | **brave** | *good* | *brave* |

un brave homme
a good man

un homme **brave**
a brave man

| | **certain** | *some* | *certain* |

une **certaine** possibilité
some possibility

une possibilité **certaine**
a certain possibility

| | **cher** | *dear* | *expensive* |

C'est un **cher** souvenir d'enfance.
It's a dear childhood memory.

C'est un bibelot très **cher**.
It's a very expensive knick-knack.

| | **grand** | *great* | *big* |

C'est un **grand** homme.
He's a great man.

C'est un homme **grand**.
He's a big man.

| | **même** | *the same* | *. . . self* |

C'est le **même** étudiant.
It's the same student.

C'est l'étudiant lui-**même**.
It's the student himself.

| | **nouveau** | *new-different* | *new-style* |

C'est ma **nouvelle** voiture.
It's my new car.

C'est une voiture **nouvelle**.
It's a new car.

| | **pauvre** | *unfortunate* | *poor* |

Pauvre poète!
Poor poet!

C'est un poète **pauvre**.
He's a poor poet.

| | **propre** | *own* | *clean* |

C'est ma **propre** histoire.
It's my own story.

Ma chemise est **propre**.
My shirt is clean.

| | **seul** | *only one* | *alone, lonely* |

C'est le **seul** homme ici.
He's the only man here.

C'est un homme **seul**.
He's a lonely man.

	precedes	follows
unique	*only*	*unique*

C'est l'**unique** étudiante hollandaise
dans la salle.
*She's the only Dutch student in
the room.*

C'est un étudiant **unique!**
He's a unique student!

vieux	*old (long-time)*	*elderly*

C'est mon **vieil** ami François.
It's my long-time friend François.

C'est mon ami, le **vieux** François.
It's my friend, old François.

3-2 Numerical adjectives *express number and order.*

✔ Numerical adjectives are either cardinal or ordinal. They precede the noun.

3-2a Cardinal numbers do not agree in gender with the noun they modify, with the exception of **un**.

Ce roman a deux cent cinquante et une pages.
This novel has 251 pages.

✔ The numbers **vingt** and **cent** add an -s when they make up more than one unit of twenty or one hundred.

quatre-vingts (80 = 4 × 20) trois cents (3 × 100)

✔ *But* an -s is not added when **vingt** and **cent** are followed by another number.

quatre-vingt-treize (93)   trois cent deux (302)

3-2b Ordinal numbers express order.

premier(ère)	deuxième	troisième	quatrième	cinquième
first	*second*	*third*	*fourth*	*fifth*

3-3 Possessive adjectives *are modifiers denoting possession.*

possessor	single possession		plural possession	
	masculine	feminine	masculine/feminine	
je	**mon**	**ma**	**mes**	*my*
tu	**ton**	**ta**	**tes**	*your*
il/elle/on	**son**	**sa**	**ses**	*his/her/its*
nous	**notre**	**notre**	**nos**	*our*
vous	**votre**	**votre**	**vos**	*your*
ils/elles	**leur**	**leur**	**leurs**	*their*

✔ In front of a vowel or a mute **h**, use **mon, ton,** and **son** instead of **ma, ta, sa** to introduce a feminine noun.

mon ami
my friend (male)

mon amie
my friend (female)

son arbre
his/her tree

ton hôtel
your hotel

Mon amie Pierrette, **ton** audace m'étonne.
Pierrette, my friend, your audacity amazes me.

Son haleine est terrible.
His/her breath is terrible.

✔ Possessive adjectives must agree in number and gender with the nouns modified.

✔ When **son, sa,** and **ses** are used, there is only one possessor of one or more things.

le vélo à Pierre: **son** vélo
Pierre's bike   *his bike*
la voiture à Marie: **sa** voiture
Marie's car   *her car*
les livres à Jany: **ses** livres
Jany's books   *her books*

✔ When **leur** and **leurs** are used, there is more than one possessor of one or more things.

Leur maison est belle. (La maison à Loulou et Fannou).
Their house is beautiful.

Leurs enfants sont beaux. (Les enfants à Loulou et Fannou).
Their children are beautiful.

✔ Possessive adjectives are repeated before each noun in a series.

Mon père, **ma** mère et **ma** soeur sont allés au théâtre.
My father, mother, and sister went to the theater.

✔ When there is no doubt about the possessor, the definite article is used instead of the possessive adjective with the parts of the body.

Elle a **les** mains sales.
Her hands are dirty.

✔ When there is doubt about who the possessor is, if the body part is modified by an adjective or another expression, or if the body part is the subject of the sentence, the possessive adjective is used.

Montre-moi **tes** pieds.   **Tes** mains sont propres.
Show me your feet.   *Your hands are clean.*

mes grandes oreilles
my big ears

The exceptions are with the adjectives **droite** and **gauche**.

J'ai l'oreille gauche toute rouge.
My left ear is totally red.

✔ Possessive adjectives are also used in several idiomatic expressions.

avoir **son** permis de conduire   passer **son** bac
to have your driver's license   *to take your high school exit exam*

faire **sa** toilette   prendre **son** temps
to wash up   *to take your time*

faire **son** service militaire
to serve in the military

3-4 Demonstrative adjectives *point out a specific person, place, thing, or idea and distinguish it from others of the same class, or refer back to a noun already mentioned.*

Il était une fois une petite fille; **cette** fille . . .
Once upon a time there was a little girl; this little girl . . .

singular	masculine	feminine
this, that	ce (cet)	cette
plural		
these, those	ces	ces

✔ Demonstrative adjectives must agree in gender and number with the nouns they modify. In English they correspond to **this, that** (singular: masculine or feminine) **these,** and **those** (plural: masculine or feminine).

✔ **Cet** is used before a masculine singular noun beginning with a vowel or mute **h.**

cet homme	**cet** appartement
this man	*this apartment*

✔ To make a direct comparison between two elements, add **-ci** and **-là** after the nouns to emphasize the contrast.

Ce tableau-**ci** est extraordinaire à la différence de ce tableau-**là**.
This picture here is extraordinary, unlike that picture over there.

✔ To clarify the distance in time or space of the speaker from the object, attach **-ci** or **-là** to the end of the modified noun.

-ci	*this*	-là	*that*

Cette maison-**ci** est moins belle que cette maison-**là**.
This house is less pretty than that house.

3-5 Interrogative adjectives *are used to ask questions in order to identify one person, thing, or a group of persons or things from a larger group.*

singular	masculine	feminine
	quel	quelle
plural		
	quels	quelles

✔ Interrogative adjectives must agreee in gender and number with the nouns they modify.

Quelle maison?	**Quel** cahier préferes-tu?
Which house?	*Which notebook do you prefer?*

✔ Interrogative adjectives may be separated from the nouns they modify when used with **être.**

Quelle est la maison de ta famille?
Which is your family's house?

✔ **Quel** is also used in exclamations, agreeing in gender and number with the noun modified.

Quel culot!	**Quelle** audace!
What nerve!	*What audacity!*

3-6 Indefinite adjectives *refer to an undefined quantity of things or beings. Indefinite adjectives are more indeterminate and imprecise than the other adjectives of quantity.*

aucun(e)	autre	certain(e)	chaque	même
any	*other*	*some*	*each, every*	*same*
nul(le)	plusieurs	quelque	tel(le)	tout/e
not one	*several*	*some, a few*	*such*	*all*

Je n'ai **aucune** nouvelle de lui.
I don't have any news of him.

Vous n'avez jamais vécu une **telle** aventure.
You have never lived through such an adventure.

Chaque matin il lit le journal.
Every morning he reads the newspaper.

3-7 Comparisons of equality and inequality *are used to compare two persons or things.*

CHART 7	COMPARISONS OF ADJECTIVES OR ADVERBS

SUPERIORITY	INFERIORITY	EQUALITY
plus + adjective or adverb + **que**	**moins** + adjective or adverb + **que**	**aussi** + adjective or adverb + **que**
more *than*	*less* *than*	*as* *as*

Before numbers, **que** is expressed by **de**.

Il est **plus** chic **que** son père.
He is more stylish than his father.

Ils sont **aussi** heureux **que** leurs parents.
They are as happy as their parents.

Je cours **plus** vite **que** toi.
I run faster than you.

Elle est **moins** belle **que** sa fille.
She is less beautiful than her daughter.

Je lui ai prêté **plus de** dix livres.
I lent him more than ten books.

✔ The adjectives **bon** and **mauvais** have irregular comparative forms.

bon	meilleur(e)/meilleur(e)s	*better*
mauvais	plus mauvais(e)/mauvaises	*worse*
	pire	*worse*
petit	petit(e)/petites	*smaller in terms of size or measure*
	moindre(s)	*less in terms of value or importance*

Cet hôtel est **meilleur** que l'autre.
This hotel is better than the other.

Le rémède est **pire** que le mal.
The medicine is worse than the illness.

Cette maison est **plus petite** que la mienne.
This house is smaller than mine.

Ses problèmes financiers sont **moindres** que ses problèmes familiaux.
His financial problems are less important than his family problems.

✔ The adverbs **bien** and **mal** also have irregular forms.

bien   mieux
well   *better*

mal   plus mal, pis
badly   *worse*

Il joue mieux que moi.
He plays better than I.

✔ Some adjectives are used without comparative signs (**plus, moins,** etc . . .) because they are already comparative in nature.

supérieur	≠	inférieur
antérieur	≠	postérieur
extérieur	≠	intérieur
majeur	≠	mineur
plus	≠	moindre

Comparison of verbs

✔ To compare people's actions, use **plus, moins, autant, mieux,** and **pis** after the verb.

Il mange **plus** (+) *que moi.*
He eats more than I.

Il mange **autant** (=) que moi.
He eats as much as I.

Il mange **moins** (−) que moi.
He eats less than I.

Comparison of nouns

✔ **Plus de, autant de** and **moins de + noun + que** are used to compare the quantity of something.

J'ai **autant de** livres que toi.
I have as many books as you.

Il a mangé **plus de** bananes que de prunes.
He ate more bananas than plums.

3-8 Superlatives *are used to compare one or several persons or things to the rest of the group.*

✔ Superlatives express the idea of the most, the least, the best, and the worst.

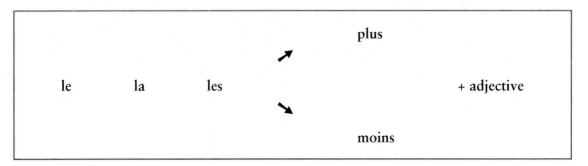

Paris est **la plus belle** ville du monde.
Paris is the most beautiful city in the world.

C'est **le moins intéressant** de ses romans.
It is the least interesting of his novels.

✔ If the superlative follows the noun, the definite article is repeated.

C'est **le** garçon **le** plus doux du monde.
He's the sweetest boy in the world.

✔ If the noun follows the superlative, the definite article **le** doesn't change.

C'est Marie qui a **le** plus d'idées.
It is Marie who has the most ideas.

✔ Some superlative adjectives are used without the comparative or superlative signs (**plus, moins, le plus, le moins,** etc. . . .) because they are already superlative: **suprême, ultime, excellent, infini,** and **immense.**

3-9 The absolute superlative *is used to denote a high degree of quality without directly comparing the person or thing to anybody or anything else.*

✔ The absolute superlative is formed by using an adverb to modify the adjective, such as **très, tout à fait, fort, bien,** etc.

C'est **très** facile.   C'est **fort** probable.
It is very easy.   *It is very probable.*

Il est **tout à fait** exemplaire.
He is quite a model.

CHAPTER 4

Adverbs

Adverbs are words that qualify or modify verbs, adjectives, or other adverbs. They do not change forms.

✔ Adverbs express time, place, manner, degree, affirmation, or negation.

✔ When adverbs modify adjectives and other adverbs, they are placed before the modified adjective or adverb.

Il est **très** beau.
He is very handsome.

✔ When adverbs modify a verb, they are placed after the **verb**, or after **pas, plus,** or **jamais** in a negative sentence.

Je n'aime pas **beaucoup** la viande.
I don't like meat very much.

✔ Short adverbs in a compound tense are placed between the auxiliary verb and the past participle.

Les critiques ont **bien** aimé le roman.
The critics really liked the novel.

✔ *But* adverbs of time and place such as, **aujourd'hui, demain, hier, ici, là, tôt,** and **tard** are placed after the past participle in a compound tense.

Elle est arrivée **tard**.   Il est arrivé **tôt** ce matin
She arrived late.   *He arrived early this morning.*

Il est parti **loin d'ici** à la recherche d'un emploi.
He went far away in search of a job.

✔ When the verb is followed by an infinitive, the adverb precedes the infinitive.

Elle va **beaucoup** aimer ce roman.
She is going to like that novel a lot.

4-1 **Adverbs of manner** *show how something is done or happens.*

✔ Adverbs of manner are formed by adding the suffix **-ment** to the feminine singular form of adjectives that end in a consonant. The suffix **-ment** is the suffix *-ly* in English.

✔ Adverbs of manner answer the question **comment?** (*how?*)

froid	froide	$\rightarrow$	froide**ment**
			coldly
frais	fraîche	$\rightarrow$	fraîche**ment**
			freshly

Some exceptions are **gentiment, brièvement, obscurément.**

✔ If the adjective ends in **i, é, e,** or **u,** the suffix **-ment** is added to the masculine form of the adjective.

vrai	$\rightarrow$	vrai**ment**	aisé	$\rightarrow$	aisé**ment**
facile	$\rightarrow$	facile**ment**	absolu	$\rightarrow$	absolu**ment**

Some exceptions are **énormément, intensément, précisément, [follement].**

✔ If the adjective ends in **-ant,** drop **-ant** and add **-amment.**

courant $\rightarrow$ cour**amment**

✔ If the adjective ends in **-ent** drop **-ent** and add **-emment.**

évident $\rightarrow$ évid**emment**

An exception is **lentement.**

✔ Adverbs of manner are generally placed after the verb.

Comme d'habitude elle me regardait **froidement**, presque avec haine.
As always, she looked at me coldly, almost with hate.

✔ Adverbs of manner can be placed at the beginning of a sentence for emphasis.

Lentement l'auteur avançait vers la vieille serrant le couteau dans sa main gauche.
Slowly the author approached the old lady, grasping the knife in his left hand.

✔ Some adverbs of manner are formed with a noun.

bête	bêtement
beast	*stupidly*

✔ Some other adverbs of manner follow:

Bien means **très** in front of an adjective or adverb.

Elle est **bien** malade.
She is very sick.

Bien means **beaucoup** in front of a noun or in front of **d'autres.**

Bien d'autres ont vu ce film.
Many others saw this movie.

Bien means *well* after a verb.

Il parle **bien** le français.
He speaks French well.

Mal means *poorly* when it appears after a verb.

Il parle **mal** l'espagnol.
He speaks Spanish poorly.

Pis is the comparative of **mal.**

Il va de **mal** en **pis** ce garçon.
This boy is going from bad to worse.

✔ **Comme** can be used to mean *as.*

Il parle **comme** un roi.
He speaks like a king.

Some other adverbs of manner follow.

ainsi	à tort	plutôt
thus	*wrongly*	*rather*
exprès	vite	volontiers
on purpose	*quickly*	*willingly*

4-2 Adverbs of time *tell when the action or event occurs.*

✔ Adverbs of time answer the question **quand?** (*when?*).

hier	avant-hier	aujourd'hui	demain
yesterday	*the day before yesterday*	*today*	*tomorrow*
après-demain	maintenant	aussitôt	longtemps
the day after tomorrow	*now*	*as soon as*	*for a long time*
autrefois	jadis	naguère	désormais
previously, formerly	*a long time ago*	*not long ago*	*from now on*
toujours	souvent	quelquefois, parfois	soudainement
always	*often*	*sometimes*	*suddenly*
rarement	continuellement, sans arrêt	d'abord	ensuite
rarely	*continuously*	*first*	*next*

tout de suite *at once*	encore *again, still*	tôt *early*	tard *late*
bientôt *soon*	puis *then*	déjà *already*	alors *then*
enfin *finally*	depuis *since*	plus tôt *earlier*	

D'abord j'irai à Paris, **ensuite** j'irai à Rome et **enfin** j'irai à Madrid.
First, I will go to Paris, then to Rome, and finally to Madrid.

✔ **Plus tôt** means *earlier.*

Il est rentré **plus tôt.**
He came back earlier.

✔ Do not confuse **plus tôt** with **plutôt,** meaning *rather* or *instead.*

Ne viens pas ce soir, mais **plutôt** demain matin.
Do not come tonight, but tomorrow instead.

4-3 Adverbs of place *locate the action or event in space.*

✔ Adverbs of place answer the question **where?**

Où?   *where?*

Où es-tu?
Where are you?

Où vas-tu?
Where are you going?

Par où . . . ?   *Where . . . by?*

Par où est-il-passé?
Where did he pass by?

D'où . . . ?   *Where . . . from?*

D'où viens-tu?
Where are you coming from?

4-3a Some adverbs of place

ici *here*	là *there*	là-bas *over there*	
au-dessus de *above*	au-dessous de *below, underneath*	dessus *above*	dessous *under, underneath, beneath*
en avant *forward*	en arrière *backwards*	devant *in front*	derrière *behind, in back of*
loin *far*	près *near*	dedans *inside*	dehors *outside*
ailleurs *elsewhere*	partout *everywhere*		

4-3b *y* and *en* denoting place

✔ The adverb y means **dans cet endroit** *(in that place)*. It replaces a noun denoting place introduced by the preposition à.

Il est **à la fac?** *Is he at the college?*	Oui, il **y** est. *Yes, he is there.*
Allez **au restaurant!** *Go to the restaurant!*	Allez-**y**! *Go there!*
N'allez pas **au restaurant!** *Do not go to the restaurant!*	N'**y** allez pas! *Do not go there!*

✔ The adverb **en** means **de cet endroit** *(from that place)*. It replaces a noun denoting place introduced by the preposition **de**.

Il vient **de la fac?** *Is he returning from the college?*	Oui, il **en** vient. *Yes, he is returning from there.*
Ils reviennent **de Paris.** *They are returning from Paris.*	Ils **en** reviennent. *They are returning from there.*

4-4 Adverbs of quantity *determine amount or quantity.*

✔ Adverbs of quantity answer the questions **combien?** *(How much? or How many?)*

combien *how many (much)*	assez *enough*	autant *as much, as many*	beaucoup *much, many*
bien *many*	davantage *more*	guère *hardly*	moins *less*
peu, un peu *a little*	plus *more*	si *so*	tant *so much*
tellement *so, so much*	tout *totally, very*	très *very*	trop *too much*

*The adverb **tout** does not change forms except before a feminine adjective beginning in a consonant or aspirated **h.**

Elle était **toute** surprise, **toute** honteuse et **tout** intimidée.
She was completely surprised, completely ashamed, and completely intimidated.

✔ The adverb **beaucoup** is used with a verb, a comparative, or with a noun preceded by **de.**

Elle a **beaucoup** voyagé.
She has traveled a lot.

Elle voyage **beaucoup plus que** son mari.
She travels much more than her husband.

Elle fait **beaucoup de** voyages.
She travels a lot.

✔ **Peu** is used with a verb or a noun preceded by **de.**

Elle a mangé **peu de** fruits.
She ate a few fruits.

Elle fait **peu de** voyages.
She travels little.

✔ The adverb **très** is used with an adjective or an adverb.

Il est **très** sympathique.
He is very nice.

Il va **très** bien.
He is doing very well.

Très does not mean the same thing as **trop.**

La soupe est **très** chaude.
The soup is very hot.

La soupe est **trop** chaude.
The soup is too hot.

✔ **Tant, si,** and **tellement** are adverbs of quantity that express exageration.

Il fait **si** mauvais aujourd'hui!
The weather is so bad today!

J'ai **tellement** faim!
I am so hungry!

4-4a Adverbial phrases that show comparisons are **plus . . . que, moins . . . que, autant . . . que,** and **aussi . . . que.**

✔ The adverb **autant** is always used with a verb or before a noun preceded by **de.**

Il a écrit **autant** de livres **que** toi.
He has written as many books as you.

✔ The adverb *aussi* is always used with an adjective or an adverb.

Il est **aussi** intelligent **qu'**elle.
He is as intelligent as she is.

4-5 Adverbs of doubt, affirmation, and negation

Doubt			
apparemment	peut-être	probablement	
apparently	*maybe*	*probably*	
Affirmation			
oui	si	bien sûr	certainement
yes	*yes*	*of course*	*certainly*
parfaitement	sans doute	soit	
perfectly	*certainly, without a doubt*	*very well*	
Negation			
non	ne . . . pas	pas du tout	nullement
no	*no*	*not at all*	*not at all*
jamais	personne	rien	
never	*nobody*	*nothing, no one*	

4-6 Interrogative adverbs

où?	comment?	pourquoi?	quand?	combien?
where?	*how?*	*why?*	*when?*	*how many?, how much?*

4-7 Negative sentences

✔ You must use two negative adverbs to make a sentence negative: **ne,** which is always placed in front of the verb, and **pas, jamais, rien,** etc.

✔ **Ne** contracts in front of a verb beginning with a vowel or mute *h*.

Je **n'**habite **pas** ici.
I don't live here.

Ils **ne** sont **jamais** là.
They are never there.

Il fait beau, **n'est**-ce pas?
It's nice out, isn't it?

Tu le connais? **Non,** je **ne** le connais **pas**.
Do you know him? No, I don't know him.

simple tenses

ne + verb + pas
Je **ne** parlerai **pas**.
I will not speak.

compound tenses

ne + auxiliary verb + pas + past participle or **infinitive**
Marie **ne s'est pas lavé** les mains.
Marie didn't wash her hands.

Marie **ne va pas se laver** les mains.
Marie is not going to wash her hands.

infinitive

ne pas + infinitive
Je vous conseille de **ne pas fumer**.
I advise you not to smoke.

✔ In a question using an inverted subject and verb, **ne** is placed before the verb and **pas** follows the subject pronoun.

N'êtes-vous **pas** de notre avis?
Don't you agree with us?

CHART 8 ADVERBS

MANNER	TIME	PLACE	QUANTITY
Add **-ment** to the feminine form of the adjective. If the masculine form ends in **i, é, e, u**, add **-ment**.	alors *then*	au-dessus ≠ au-dessous *above ≠ below*	combien *how many, how much*
à tort *wrongly*	après-demain *the day after tomorrow*	ailleurs *elsewhere*	assez *enough*
ainsi *thus*	aujourd'hui *today*	dedans ≠ dehors *inside ≠ outside*	autant *as much, as many*
bien *well*	aussitôt *as soon as*	dessus ≠ dessous *on (top of), over, above ≠ underneath, under, beneath*	beaucoup *much, many*
bien *very*	autrefois *previously, formerly*	devant ≠ derrière *in front of ≠ behind, in back of*	bien *many*
exprès *on purpose*	avant-hier *the day before yesterday*	en avant ≠ en arrière *forward ≠ backwards*	davantage *more*
mal *badly*	d'abord *first*	ici ≠ là *here ≠ there*	guère *hardly*
plutôt *rather*	demain *tomorrow*	là-bas *over there*	moins *less*
très *very*	depuis *since*	loin ≠ près *far ≠ near*	peu, un peu *a little*
vite *quickly*	désormais *from now on*	partout *everywhere*	plus *more*
volontiers *willingly*	encore *again, still*		tant *so much*
	ensuite *next*		tellement, si *so*
	hier *yesterday*		tout *totally*
	jadis *along time ago*		très *very*
	longtemps *for a long time*		trop *too much*

CHART 8   ADVERBS, CONTINUED

MANNER	TIME	PLACE	—
doubt	maintenant	**affirmation**	
apparemment	*now*	oui	
apparently		*yes*	
	naguère		
peut-être	*not long ago*	si	
maybe		*yes*	
	puis		
probablement	*then*	certainement	
probably		*certainly*	
	quelquefois,		
negation	parfois	sans doute	
non	*sometimes*	*without a doubt*	
no			
	rarement	bien sûr	
pas du tout	*rarely, seldom*	*of course*	
not at all			
	continuellement,	parfaitement	
jamais	sans arrêt	*perfectly*	
never	*continuously*		
		soit	
rien	soudainement	*very well*	
nothing	*suddenly*		
ne . . . pas	souvent		
no	*often*		
nullement	tard		
not at all	*late*		
personne	tôt		
nobody, no one	*early*		
	toujours		
	always		
	tout de suite		
	at once		

CHAPTER 5

Pronouns

Pronouns are words used as a substitute for a noun.

5-1 Personal pronouns *are used in place of a noun or group of words already mentioned, to avoid repetition.*

✔ Personal pronouns can be used as a subject, direct or indirect object of a verb, or as an object of a preposition.

CHART 9	PERSONAL PRONOUNS	

SUBJECT	DIRECT OBJECT	INDIRECT OBJECT
je *I*	**me/m'** *me*	**me/m'** *(to, for) me*
tu *you* *(informal)*	**te/t'** *you* *(informal)*	**te/t'** *(to, for) you* *(informal)*
vous *you* *(singular, formal)*	**vous** *you* *(formal)*	**vous** *(to, for) you* *(formal)*
il/elle *he, she*	**le/la/l'** *him, her*	**lui** *(to, for) him, her*
on *one, you (general sense), we*		
nous *we*	**nous** *us*	**nous** *(to, for) us*
vous *you* *(plural)*	**vous** *you* *(plural)*	**vous** *(to, for) you*
ils/elles *they (masc., fem.)*	**les** *them*	**leur** *(to, for) them*

CHART 9   PERSONAL PRONOUNS, CONTINUED

STRESSED	REFLEXIVE
moi *me, myself*	**me** *(to) myself*
toi *you, yourself (informal)*	**te** *(to) yourself (informal)*
vous *you, yourself (formal)*	**vous** *(to) yourself (formal)*
lui/elle/soi *him, himself, her, herself one, oneself*	**se** *(to) him, himself her, herself one, oneself*
nous *us, ourselves*	**nous** *(to) ourselves*
vous *you, yourselves (plural)*	**vous** *(to) yourselves*
eux/elles *them, themselves (masc., fem.)*	**se** *(to) themselves*

5-2 Subject pronouns *identify who performs the action and are used to refer to people and things.*

singular	plural
je *I*	**nous** *we*
tu, vous *you (informal, formal)*	**vous** *you (plural)*
il/elle/on *he, she, one, you (general use), we*	**ils/elles** *they (masc., fem.)*

✔ Before a verb beginning with a vowel or mute **h**, **je** changes to **j'** . . .

J'habite rue Saint-Honoré.
I live on Saint-Honoré Street.

✔ Subject pronouns are usually placed before the verb.

✔ Subject pronouns are the subject of the verb.

Elle prend son petit déjeuner.   **Il** ne prend pas de café.
She eats her breakfast.   *He doesn't drink coffee.*

Ces plantes sont magnifiques et **elles** poussent partout.
These plants are magnificent, and they grow everywhere.

✔ **Il** becomes a neutral pronoun when used in impersonal sentences.

Il fait chaud.   **Il** neige.
It is hot.   *It is snowing.*

✔ When using inversion for an interrogative sentence, subject pronouns may follow the simple verb.

Ecrivez-**vous** des romans d'amour?
Do you write romance novels?

✔ When using inversion in a compound tense, subject pronouns follow the auxiliary verb.

As-**tu** lu son dernier roman?
Did you read his last novel?

5-3 Direct Object Pronouns *refer to direct objects; nouns referring to persons or things that directly receive the action of the verb and are not attached to the verb by a preposition.*

singular	plural
*me	nous
me	*us*
*te	*vous
you (informal)	*you (formal, plural)*
*vous	
you (formal)	
**le/la	**les
him, her, it	*them*

*refers to people   **refers to people or things

✔ Direct object pronouns replace a noun that follows a transitive verb and completes the meaning or receives the action of the verb. The noun is usually preceded by a definite or indefinite article, a possessive, or a demonstrative adjective.

As-tu rencontré Jean?   Non, je ne l'ai pas rencontré.
Did you meet Jean?   *No, I didn't meet him.*

Il achètera cette voiture.   Il l'achètera.
He will buy this car.   *He will buy it.*

✔ Direct object pronouns answer the question **whom?** or **what?**

Elle a lu **le livre**.   Elle l'a lu.
She read the book.   *She read it.*

Vous m'avez-vu?	Oui, je **vous** *ai vu.*
Did you see me?	*Yes, I saw you.*

✔ Direct object pronouns must agree in gender and number with the nouns they replace. In simple tenses, direct object pronouns are placed before the conjugated verb.

Elle lit **les livres.**	Elle **les** lit.
She reads the books.	*She reads them.*

✔ In sentences with a past participle, direct object pronouns are placed before the auxiliary verb.

Je ne **l'**ai pas encore lu.
I have not read it yet.

✔ In an affirmative command, direct object pronouns follow the verb and are attached with a hyphen.

Etudiez-**le!**	Invite-**moi!**
Study it!	*Invite me!*

After an affirmative command, **me** becomes **moi,** and **te** becomes **toi.**

✔ Direct object pronouns are placed before the verb in negative commands.

Ne **l'**étudiez pas!	Ne **me** parlez pas d'amour!
Don't study it!	*Don't talk to me about love!*

✔ When a verb is followed by an infinitive, direct object pronouns are placed before the infinitive.

Vous devez faire une composition.	Vous devez **la** faire.
You must write a composition.	*You must write it.*

✔ Direct object pronouns can be used with **voici** and **voilà.**

Le (la) voici.	**Le (la)** voilà.
Here he (she) is.	*There he (she) is.*

✔ In front of words beginning with a **vowel** or mute **h,** the singular forms of direct object pronouns become **m', t', l'.**

Il écrit **un nouveau roman.**	Il **l'**écrit.
He is writing a new novel.	*He is writing it.*

5-4 Indirect object pronouns *replace an indirect object noun and tell to whom or for whom the action of the verb is done.*

singular	plural
me	**nous**
to (for) me	*to (for) us*
te /vous	**vous**
to (for) you (informal/formal)	*to (for) you*
lui	**leur**
to (for) him/her	*to (for) them*

✔ Indirect object pronouns are always introduced by the preposition **à.**

Some particular cases:

after **être à quelqu'un, penser à quelqu'un, songer à quelqu'un, rêver à quelqu'un, tenir à quelqu'un** . . . and after reflexive verbs followed by the preposition à, (**s'intéreser à, s'attacher à, s'adresser à** . . .), when the stressed pronouns **moi, toi, lui, elle, nous, vous, eux,** and **elles** are used.

Je songe à **elle.**	Je m'intéresse à **eux.**
I dream of her.	*I'm interested in them.*

✔ Indirect object pronouns share the same form as direct object pronouns except in the third-person singular, **lui,** and in the third-person plural, **leur.**

✔ **Lui** and **leur** refer only to persons. However, they are used for both male and female.

Je parle à ma fille.	Je **lui** parle.
I talk to my daughter.	*I talk to her.*
Je parle à mes enfants.	Je **leur** parle.
I talk to my children.	*I talk to them.*

✔ Direct and indirect object pronouns are placed before the verb except in an affirmative command, where they are placed after the verb, attached with a hyphen.

Ils offrent des fleurs à leurs amies.
They give flowers to their friends.

Ils **les leur** offrent.	Offrez-**les leur!**
They give them to them.	*Give them to them!*

✔ In negative commands, object pronouns come after **ne.**

Ne **le leur** donnez pas!
Don't give it to them!

✔ *Attention!* Some French verbs followed by **à** are often not introduced by *to* in English: **téléphoner à, dire à, demander à, offrir à, plaire à.** In fact, some French verbs take a direct object, while their English counterparts require a preposition.

attendre	demander	écouter
to wait for	*to ask for*	*to listen to*
espérer	regarder	payer
to hope for	*to look at*	*to pay for*
chercher		
to look for		

5-5 **Reflexive pronouns** *indicate that the subject of a verb does something to himself, herself, or themselves. The subject of the action is also the recipient of the action. Reflexive pronouns generally take forms of direct object pronouns.*

singular	plural
me≠m'	**nous**
to myself	*to ourselves*
te/t' vous	**vous**
to yourself (informal/formal)	*to yourselves*
se≠s'	**se≠s'**
to him/herself	*to themselves*

✔ Reflexive pronouns are used to make a verb reflexive. For the conjugation of reflexive verbs, see appendix of verbs: 50, 51, and 52; pages 153–154.

Pierre couche ses enfants à sept heures.	Pierre **se** lève tôt et **se** couche tard.
Pierre puts his children to bed at seven.	*Pierre gets up early and goes to bed late.*

✔ Reflexive pronouns are indirect objects when the reflexive verb is followed by a direct object, or is used to show a reciprocal action. explain:... a reciprocal action. In this case there will be no agreement since the direct object doesn't precede the verb.

Examples:

ils **se** sont lav**és**	ils se sont lavé **les mains**
they washed themselves	*they washed their hands*
Pierre s'est acheté **une chemise.**	Marie s'est brossé **les dents.**
Pierre bought himself a shirt.	*Marie brushed her teeth.*

Ils **se** sont téléphoné et ils **se** sont parlé pendant deux heures.
They called each other and talked (to each other) for two hours.

5-6 The pronouns *y* and *en*

✔ Use **y** to replace a noun that is preceded by **à** when the noun refers to a thing or idea.

Pensez-vous **à la question**?   Oui, j'**y** pense.
Are you thinking about the question?   *Yes, I'm thinking about it.*

✔ Use **y** to replace a noun referring to a place preceded by any preposition other than **de**. (**à, à côté de, dans, en, en face de, près de, derrière, devant, entre, en face de, sous, sur, chez**)

Il est **dans** sa chambre?   Oui, il **y** est.
Is he in his room?   *Yes, he is there.*

Je vais **à Paris**.   J'**y** vais.
I'm going to Paris.   *I'm going there.*

✔ The pronoun **y** is omitted before the future and conditional forms of the verb **aller**.

Vous irez en Europe?   Oui, j'irai en été.
Will you go to Europe?   *Yes, I will go in the summer.*

✔ Use **en** to replace a noun referring to a thing or idea that is preceded by **de**.

Tu as beaucoup **de projets**?   Tu **en** as beaucoup?
Do you have a lot of projects?   *Do you have a lot of them?*

Vous avez **de l'argent**?   Oui, j'**en** ai un peu.
Do you have money?   *Yes, I have some.*

✔ Use **en** also to replace a noun referring to a place that is preceded by **de**.

Marie sort **de la Comédie Française**.
Marie is leaving the Comédie Française.

Elle **en** sort.
She is leaving there.

✔ En also replaces a noun preceded by **du, de la, de l', des** or any expression of quantity like **un(une), deux, un peu de, plusieurs, assez de, quelques,** beaucoup de, etc.

✔ En means *of it, of them, some,* or *any.*

Il achète **du pain**.   Il **en** achète.
He is buying some bread.   *He is buying some.*

Tu as assez **de pain**?   Non, je n'**en** ai pas assez.
Do you have enough bread?   *No, I don't have enough (of it).*

✔ En and y are placed before the verb except in affirmative commands.

Il m'**en** a toujours parlé.   Allons-**y** tout de suite!
He always spoke to me about that.   *Let's go there immediately!*

✔ When a conjugated verb is followed by an infinitive, **en** and **y** precede the infinitive

Je vais **y** aller demain.
I will go there tomorrow.

✔ Y and **en** are never used together except in the expression **il y a** where **en** precedes the verb.

Il y **en** a.	Il n'y **en** a pas.	Y **en** a-t-il?
There are some.	*There are not any.*	*Are there any?*

CHART 10	PRONOUN ORDER WHEN MULTIPLE PRONOUNS ARE USED						
–	1	2	3	4	5	–	–
ne	me te se nous vous	le la les	lui leur	y	en	verb	**pas**

✔ In compound tenses, **pas** is placed immediately after the auxiliary verb.

Note: Columns 1&3, 3&4 and 4&5 can never be used together, except for **il y en a.**

Il ne **me le** donne pas.	Il ne **me l'**a pas donné.
He isn't giving it to me.	*He didn't give it to me.*

✔ When a conjugated verb is followed by an infinitive, the pronouns precede the infinitive.

Elle va **te le** donner demain.	Je ne veux pas **le lui** rendre.
She will give it to you tomorrow.	*I don't want to give it back to her.*

affirmative imperative
2 possible combinations

	dir. obj. pron.	ind. obj. pron.		ind. obj. pron.	
verb	le la les	moi toi lui nous vous leur	verb	m' t' lui nous vous leur	en
verb → direct object pronoun indirect object pronoun					

✔ In an affirmative command, object pronouns are placed after the verb, attached with a hyphen.

Etudiez-**la**!	Allez-**y**!	Donnez-**le-moi**!	Allez-**vous en**!
Study it!	*Go there!*	*Give it to me!*	*Leave!*

✔ In a negative command, object pronouns are placed before the verb.

Ne **l'**étudiez pas!	N'**y** allez pas!
Don't study it!	*Don't go there!*

5-7 Disjunctive or stress pronouns *are used to emphasize the subject or object.*

singular	**plural**
moi	**nous**
me, myself	*us, ourselves*
toi	
you, yourself (informal)	
vous	**vous**
you, yourself (formal)	*you, yourselves*
lui	**eux**
him, himself	
elle	**elles**
her, herself	*them, themselves*
soi*	
one, oneself	

***soi** is an indefinite form meaning *oneself* used in connection with **on**.

On doit toujours avoir de l'argent sur **soi**.
You should always have money with you.

✔ When used to emphasize the subject, stress pronouns are placed at the beginning or at the end of the sentence.

Moi? Je suis française, **moi**.
Me? I'm French.

✔ Stress pronouns are placed at the end of the sentence to emphasize the subject.

Pierre est un bon étudiant, **lui**.
Pierre is a good student.

✔ Stress pronouns are used after **c'est** and **ce sont**.

C'est nous.	**Ce sont** eux.
It's us.	*It's them.*

✔ Stress pronouns can be used alone as a one-word answer.

Qui est là?
Who is there?

Moi.	Lui.	Elle.	Nous.
I.	*He.*	*She.*	*We.*

✔ Stress pronouns are used in conjunction with **-même**.

Il s'est habillé **lui-même**.
He dressed himself.

J'ai réparé ma voiture **moi-même**.
I fixed my car by myself.

✔ After **et, ou, ni,** or **a preposition,** use a stress pronoun.

Pierre **et** moi.
Pierre and I.

Qui? Marie **ou** toi?
Who? Marie or you?

Elle pense beaucoup à lui.
She thinks about him a lot.

Ni toi **ni** moi aimons les glaces.
Neither you nor I like ice cream.

5-8 The neuter pronoun *le*

✔ Use **le** as a neuter pronoun to replace an adjective, a clause, or a whole sentence.

✔ Le means *it* or *so*.

Croyez-vous que la criminalité va diminuer?
Do you think crime will decrease?

Oui, je **le** crois.
Yes, I think so.

5-9 Demonstrative pronouns *are used in place of a noun and indicate their relation with the subject, space, and time.*

5-9a Definite demonstrative pronouns are used to single out the noun they replace. They must agree in number and gender with the noun replaced.

	singular		**plural**	
	masculine	feminine	masculine	feminine
	celui	**celle**	**ceux**	**celles**

✔ Definite demonstrative pronouns are followed by **a relative pronoun, a preposition,** or by **-ci** or **-là**.

Quelle est votre maison, **celle** de gauche ou **celle** de droite?
Which is your house, the one on the left or the one on the right?

✔ Followed by a relative pronoun, definite demonstrative pronouns can be translated as **he(she) who, the one(s) who (that), those who (that)**

Regarde le tableau, **celui dont** je t'ai parlé.
Look at the picture, the one I told you about.

✔ Followed by a preposition, definite demonstrative pronouns can be as **the one(s).**

Voici ma valise et **celle de** Marie.
Here is my suitcase, and Marie's.

✔ When definite demonstrative pronouns are followed by **-ci**, they indicate relative proximity to the speaker. When followed by **-là**, they indicate relative distance from the speaker. They can be translated as this (**that**) **one, these,** or **those.**

Ceux-ci sont mes livres.   **Celle-là** c'est ma voiture.
These (here) are my books.   *That one is my car.*

5-9b **Indefinite demonstrative pronouns** refer to a general idea, statement, or an object of unknown gender.

ceci   cela, ça
this   *that*

-**Ça** va?   -Oui, **ça** va. Et toi?
How are things going?   *Fine. And you?*

5-10 The neuter *ce*

✔ The demonstrative pronoun **ce** is generally used with **être**. It is followed by a noun, an adjective, a pronoun, or a superlative, and can be translated as **he, she, it, they, this,** or **that.**

✔ **C'est** precedes a noun accompanied by an article, adjective or any other modifier, or before a disjunctive pronoun.

C'est mon mari.   **C'est** un grand écrivain.
It's my husband.   *He is a great writer.*

✔ The neuter **ce** used with an adjective refers to an idea already mentioned.

J'ai fini d'écrire mon nouveau roman.   **C'est** merveilleux! *(finir le roman)*
I finished writing my new novel.   *That's wonderful! (finishing the novel)*

✔ Use **il est** and an adjective to introduce a new idea not mentioned before or when the antecedent is a specific person or thing.

J'ai fini d'écrire mon nouveau roman.   **Il est** merveilleux. *(le roman)*
I finished writing my new novel.   *It's wonderful! (the novel)*

✔ **Ce sont** is used with the third-person plural:

Ce sont mes professeurs.
These are my professors.

5-11 Interrogative pronouns *are used to seek information about people, actions, things, or situations.*

simple interrogative pronouns	**qui** *who(m)*	**que** *what*	**quoi** *what*	**à qui** *whose*
compound interrogative pronouns	**lequel** *auquel* *duquel* *(m., sg.)*	**laquelle** *à laquelle* *de laquelle* *(f., sg.)*	**lesquels** *auxquels* *desquels* *(m., pl.)*	**lesquelles** *auxquelles* *desquelles* *(f., pl.)*
		(which one)		*(which ones)*

✔ Use **qui** to ask about people.

When **qui** is the subject, place it at the beginning of the sentence.

Qui a lu *Le petit prince?*
Who has read The Little Prince?

When **qui** is an object, place it at the beginning of the sentence. Use either **qui** or **qui est-ce que**.

Qui avez vous rencontré à Paris?	**Qui** est-ce que vous avez rencontré à Paris?
Whom did you meet in Paris?	*Whom did you meet in Paris?*

When **qui** is the object of a preposition, the preposition becomes the first word of the question.

Avec qui est-ce que vous êtes allé en vacances?
With whom did you go on vacation?

Use **à qui** to denote ownership:

A qui est ce livre?	Il est **à Pierre**.
Whose book is this?	*It is Pierre's.*

✔ **Que** is used to ask about things, actions, or situations.

When **que** is the subject of the question, the form **qu'est-ce qui** must be used.

Qu'est-ce qui t'arrive?
What's wrong with you?

When **que** is the object of the question, use **qu'est-ce que** or inversion to form the question.

Qu'est-ce que vous avez dit?
What did you say?

Qu'avez-vous dit?
What did you say?

When **que** is the object of a preposition, use **quoi** immediately after the preposition and before **est-ce que** or the inversion.

De **quoi** tu parles?
What are you talking about?

Avec **quoi** pourrais-je ouvrir cette boîte?
What should I open this box with?

✔ The interrogative pronoun **lequel** agrees in gender and number with the noun modified.

singular		plural	
masculine	feminine	masculine	feminine
lequel	**laquelle**	**lesquels**	**lesquelles**

Quels livres?   **Lesquels?**
Which books?   *Which ones?*

Quelle table?   **Laquelle?**
Which table?   *Which one?*

✔ Lequel, lesquels and lesquelles contract with the prepositions **à** and **de**.

à + lequel	→	auquel	de + lequel	→	duquel
à + lesquels	→	auxquels	de + lesquels	→	desquels
à + lesquelles	→	auxquelles	de + lesquelles	→	desquelles

Nous allons au restaurant chinois.
We are going to the Chinese restaurant.

Auquel allez-vous?
Which one are you going to?

Je parle des pièces de Molière.
I'm talking about Molière's plays.

Desquelles parles-tu?
Which ones are you talking about?

✔ The feminine singular forms of **lequel** do not contract,

à laquelle   de laquelle

Je vais aller à la fête de Jean.
I'm going to Jean's party.

A laquelle vas-tu aller?
Which one are you going to?

Nous parlons de la fille française.
We are talking about the French girl.

De laquelle parlez-vous?
Which one are you talking about?

5-12 Relative pronouns *join two clauses to form a compound sentence.*

antecedent	subject	direct object	
person	**qui** *who*	**que** *whom*	
things	**qui** *that (which)*	**que** *that (which)*	
indeterminate	**ce qui** *what*	**ce que** *what*	**ce dont** *what*
person or things	**dont** *whose* *of whom* *of which*	**dont** *whose* *of whom* *of which*	

✔ The simple relative pronouns **qui** and **que** do not change in gender and number. They can replace names of persons or things.

✔ **Qui** and **que** join two clauses to avoid the repetition of a noun.

✔ **Qui** replaces the subject of the second sentence. **Qui** does not contract in front of a **vowel** or a mute **h**.

La fille emploie *Sans Détour*.　　　La fille est une bonne étudiante.
The girl uses Sans Détour.　　　*The girl is a good student.*

La fille **qui** emploie *Sans Détour* est une bonne étudiante.
The girl who uses Sans Détour *is a good student.*

✔ **Que** replaces the direct object of the relative clause. **Que** contracts in front of a **vowel** or mute **h**.

Jean m'a apporté un gâteau.　　　Je n'aime pas ce gâteau.
Jean brought me a cake.　　　*I don't like this cake.*

Je n'aime pas le gâteau **que** Jean m'a apporté.
I don't like the cake Jean brought me.

✔ **Ce qui, ce que,** and **ce dont** refer to ideas that do not have number or gender.

Ce qui m'embête c'est que la gloire soit arrivée si tard.
What bothers me is that the glory came so late.

On ne saura jamais **ce que** nos ennemis pensent.
We will never know what our enemies think.

On ne saura jamais **ce qu'**elle pense.　　　Tu auras **ce dont** tu as besoin.
We will never know what she thinks.　　　*Whatever you need, you will have it.*

✔ The relative pronoun **dont** (*of, about, of which, of whom, of where*) replaces a noun introduced by **de**, and is used instead of **de qui, duquel, de laquelle, desquels**, and **desquelles**.

C'est un livre intéressant.   Tout le monde parle de ce livre.
It is an interesting book.   *Everybody is talking about this book.*

C'est un livre intéressant **dont** tout le monde parle.
It is an interesting book that everybody is talking about.

5-13 Relative compound pronouns *replace a person or thing already mentioned.*

	masculine		feminine	
	singular	plural	singular	plural
object of a preposition	lequel	lesquels	laquelle	lesquelles
object of the preposition **de**	duquel	desquels	de laquelle	desquelles
object of the preposition **à**	auquel	auxquels	à laquelle	auxquelles

✔ Use **de qui** or **duquel** instead of **dont** after the compound prepositions with de, such as **à côté de, auprès de, près de, au sujet de, loin de, à l'intérieur de, au cours de, au milieu de, à cause de, au-dessus de**, etc.

Le livre **au sujet duquel** vous parlez est tout à fait extraordinaire.
The book you are talking about is absolutely extraordinary.

Les femmes **au milieu de qui** elle se sentait protégée, l'ont déçue.
The women among whom she felt protected, disappointed her.

✔ **Dont** cannot replace **de qui, duquel**, etc. after a noun introduced by a preposition showing possession.

La dame, contre les idées **de qui** (**de laquelle**) nous avons débattu, a démissionné son poste.
The lady against whose ideas we debated, resigned her position.

✔ In general, use the following after a preposition.

Qui for people

L'homme à **qui** je parle est grec.
The man I'm talking to is Greek.

Lequel for things

L'ordinateur avec **lequel** j'ai écrit mon livre est très puissant.
The computer I wrote my book with is very powerful.

Dont for both people and things

Enfin! Voici le texte **dont** nous avions besoin, écrit par l'auteur **dont** vous m'avez parlé.
At last! Here's the textbook we needed, written by the author you told me about.

5-14 Indefinite pronouns *refer to a noun in an imprecise way.*

✔ The following indefinite adjectives can function as indefinite pronouns.

aucun (e)	nul (le) autre	certain (e)
tel (le)	plusieurs	tout (e)

Some indefinite pronouns used without a noun are:

autrui	*the others*
chacun	*each one*
quelqu'un	*someone, somebody, anyone, anybody*
on	*one, people*
personne	*nobody, no one*
rien	*nothing*

Tu as des nouvelles de monsieur Martin? Non, **aucune**.
Do you have news from Mr. Martin? No, none.

5-15 Possessive pronouns *indicate possession.*

	singular	plural
one possessor	**le mien (la mienne)** *mine*	**les miens (miennes)** *mine*
	le tien (la tienne) *yours*	**les tiens (tiennes)** *yours*
	le sien (la sienne) *his, hers, its*	**les siens (siennes)** *his, hers, its*
several possessors	**le (la) nôtre** *ours*	**les nôtres** *ours*
	le (la) vôtre *yours*	**les vôtres** *yours*
	le (la) leur *theirs*	**les leurs** *theirs*

En parlant de livres, **les miens** sont meilleurs que **les vôtres**.
Speaking of books, mine are better than yours.

Mon père a quarante ans. Quel âge a **le tien**?
My father is forty years old. How old is yours?

Tes enfants sont grands: **les nôtres** sont plutôt petits.
Your children are tall, ours are rather short.

CHAPTER 6

Verbs

Verbs are words or groups of words that express action or a state of being.

✔ All French **infinitives** end in **-er, -ir, -oir,** or **-re.**

✔ Regular French verbs are conjugated by substituting endings that reflect the subject performing the action.

6-1 Use of the infinitive

✔ Infinitives may be the subject of a sentence.

Fumer est très mauvais pour la santé.
Smoking is very bad for your health.

✔ Infinitives may follow a preposition.

Après avoir étudié j'irai au cinéma.
After studying, I will go to the movies.

However, the present participle is used after the preposition **en.**

Elle a perdu son sac **en allant** au cinéma.
She lost her purse while going to the movies.

✔ Infinitives may be used as an imperative to give instructions or directions.

Ne pas **déranger.**
Do not disturb.

✔ Use infinitives in exclamations or questions to express doubt, wishes, or indignation.

Que **dire!**	Qui **croire?**	Toi, **parler** ainsi!
What can I say!	*Whom can I believe?*	*You, speaking like that!*

✔ Use infinitives after **venir de** to describe actions that have just taken place: **passé récent** (*recent past*).

Je viens d'**arriver** de Marseille.
I have just arrived from Marseille.

✔ After **aller** in the present tense, use infinitives to describe the immediate future, known as the **futur proche.**

Je vais **étudier** ce soir.
I'm going to study this afternoon.

✔ Infinitives are used after the following verbs:

aimer *to love*	aller *to go*	désirer *to desire*	détester *to hate*	devoir *to be obliged to*
écouter *to listen*	entendre *to hear*	espérer *to hope*	faire *to do, make*	faillir *to fail*
falloir *to be necessary*	laisser *to let, leave*	oser *to dare*	penser *to think*	préférer *to prefer*
pouvoir *to be able*	regarder *to look*	savoir *to know*	sembler *to seem*	souhaiter *to wish*
valoir *to be worth*	voir *to see*	vouloir *to want*		

Il a failli **tomber.**
He almost fell.

Elle doit **étudier.**
She should study.

Les enfants, il faut **se reposer** maintenant.
Children, you must rest now.

✔ Use the infinitive after verbs followed by prepositions such as the following: **aider à,** *(to help),* **apprendre à,** *(to learn),* **réussir à,** *(to succeed in),* **accepter de** *(to agree to do something),* **finir de** *(to finish doing something),* **oublier de** *(to forget to do something).*

J'apprends à conduire.
I'm learning to drive.

Nous **acceptons de travailler** pour votre compagnie.
We agree to work for your company.

6-2 The indicative *is a mood used in ordinary objective statements.*

✔ The indicative is made up of the following tenses: **présent** *(present),* **passé-composé** *(present perfect),* **imparfait** *(imperfect),* **plus-que-parfait** *(past perfect),* **passé-simple** *(preterite),* **futur** *(future),* **futur antérieur** *(future perfect).* **Tense** represents the **moment** of the speech or the action.

6-2a **The present tense** expresses actions that occur in the actual moment, immediate future, or habitually.

✔ The present tense has different meanings. In addition to the simple present, it can also express ongoing actions and it can be used to imply that an action will take place in the immediate future.

Je parle.	*I speak (as a habit).*
Je parle.	*I am speaking (right now).*
Je parle à la radio dans une heure.	*I will speak on the radio in an hour.*

✔ *Note:* reflexive verbs follow the same rules of conjugation as non-reflexive verbs, with the addition of a reflexive pronoun. See verb conjugations in Chapter 6, and reflexive pronouns on page 52.

6-2a-1 For present tense regular verbs ending in **-er,** drop the **-er** and add the endings shown below.

chanter (*to sing*)

	singular		plural
subject	**stem + ending**	**subject**	**stem + ending**
je	chant -e	nous	chant -ons
tu	chant -es	vous	chant -ez
il/elle/on	chant -e	ils/elles	chant -ent

6-2a-2 The present tense of irregular verbs ending in **-er**

✔ There is only one irregular verb ending in **-er.**

aller (*to go*)

subject	singular	subject	plural
je	vais	nous	allons
tu	vas	vous	allez
il/elle/on	va	ils/elles	vont

6-2a-3 The present tense of stem-changing verbs ending in **-er:** letter changes

✔ In general, verbs ending in **-eler** or **-eter** double the consonant in all forms but the first- and second-person plural forms.

l → ll		t → tt	
appeler → appell		jeter → jett	
(to call)		*(to throw)*	
singular	plural	singular	plural
j'**appell** e	nous **appel** ons	je **jett** e	nous **jet** ons
tu **appell** es	vous **appel** ez	tu **jett** es	vous **jet** ez
il/elle/on **appell** e	ils/elles **appell** ent	il/elle/on **jett** e	ils/elles **jett** ent

s'appeler	rappeler	jeter	rejeter
to be called (named)	*to call back*	*to throw*	*to reject*
étinceler	se rappeler	projeter	
to twinkle	*to remember*	*to project, throw*	

Exceptions are: **céler** *(to conceal, to keep secret)*, **ciseler** *(to chisel, to cut)*, **congeler** *(to freeze)*, **déceler** *(to disclose)*, **démanteler** *(to break up)*, **écarteler** *(to quarter)*, **geler** *(to freeze)*, **marteler** *(to hammer)*, **modeler** *(to model)*, **peler** *(to peel)*. These verbs replace the -e mute of the infinitive with -è.

je gèle	nous gelons
tu gèles	vous gelez
il/elle/on gèle	ils/elles gèlent

Exceptions are: **acheter** *(to buy)*, **racheter** *(to buy again)*, **crocheter** *(to pick* or *to hook)*, **fureter** *(to nose around)*, **haleter** *(to gasp)*. These verbs replace the mute e of the infinitive with a -è.

j'achète	nous achetons
tu achètes	vous achetez
il/elle/on achète	ils/elles achètent

✔ Verbs having a y → i spelling change in the singular- and the third-person plural forms appear below.

essayer* → essai
(to try)

payer* → pai
(to pay)

singular	plural	singular	plural
j'essai -e	nous essay -ons	je pai -e	nous pay -ons
tu essai -es	vous essay -ez	tu pai -es	vous pay -ez
il/elle/on essai -e	ils/elles essai -ent	il/elle/on pai -e	ils/elles pai -ent

Other verbs like **essayer** and **payer** appear below.

balayer	employer	ennuyer
to sweep	*to employ*	*to annoy*
envoyer	essuyer	nettoyer
to send	*to wipe*	*to clean*

*It is considered acceptable not to change the **y** for verbs ending in **-ayer.**

✔ Verb stems with letters that change only in the first-person plural to maintain pronunciation appear below.

$$c \rightarrow ç$$

annoncer $\rightarrow$ *annonç*		commencer $\rightarrow$ *commenç*	
(to announce)		*(to begin)*	
singular	**plural**	**singular**	**plural**
j'**annonc** -e	nous **annonç** -ons	je **commenc** -e	nous **commenç** -ons
tu **annonc** -es	vous **annonc** -ez	tu **commenc** -es	vous **commenc** -ez
il/elle/on **annonc** -e	ils/elles **annonc** -ent	il/elle/on **commenc** -e	ils/elles **commenc** -ent

Other verbs like **annoncer** and **commencer** follow.

divorcer	effacer	s'efforcer	se fiancer	menacer
to divorce	*to erase*	*to strive*	*to get engaged*	*to threaten*

$$g \rightarrow ge$$

manger		changer	
(to eat)		*(to exchange)*	
singular	**plural**	**singular**	**plural**
je **mang** -e	nous **mange** -ons	je **chang** -e	nous **change** -ons
tu **mang** -es	vous **mang** -ez	tu **chang** -es	vous **chang** -ez
il/elle/on **mang** -e	ils/elles **mang** -ent	il/elle/on **chang** -e	ils/elles **chang** -ent

Other verbs like **manger** appear below.

arranger	charger	corriger	déranger	diriger
to arrange, to fix	*to charge*	*to correct*	*to disturb*	*to direct*
exiger	interroger	juger	mélanger	nager
to demand	*to question*	*to judge*	*to mix*	*to swim*
négliger	obliger	partager	plonger	prolonger
to neglect	*to compel*	*to share*	*to dive*	*to prolong*
ranger	venger	voyager		
to put away	*to avenge*	*to travel*		

6-2a-4 The present tense of stem-changing verbs ending in -er: with accent mark changes

✔ Verbs ending in -ecer, -emer, -ener, -eper, -eser, -ever, -evrer and some verbs ending in -eler or -eter receive an accent mark to change the silent -e into an open è.

✔ Changes occur in all but the first- and second-person plural forms.

$$e \rightarrow è$$

<table>
<tr><td colspan="2">mener → mèn
(to lead)</td><td colspan="2">lever → lèv
(to lift)</td></tr>
<tr><td>singular</td><td>plural</td><td>singular</td><td>plural</td></tr>
<tr><td>je mèn -e</td><td>nous men -ons</td><td>je lèv -e</td><td>nous lev -ons</td></tr>
<tr><td>tu mèn -es</td><td>vous men -ez</td><td>tu lèv -es</td><td>vous lev -ez</td></tr>
<tr><td>il/elle/on mèn -e</td><td>ils/elles mèn -ent</td><td>il/elle/on -lèv -e</td><td>ils/elles lèv -ent</td></tr>
</table>

amener	élever	enlever	se promener
to take,	*to raise*	*to take away,*	*to take a walk*
to bring along		*to remove*	

✔ Verbs with the following endings change -é → -è in all but the first- and second-person plural forms.

-ébrer	célébrer *to celebrate*	-éger	assiéger *to besiege*	éler	révéler *to reveal*	-érer	préférer *to prefer*
-écer	rapiécer *to patch*	-égler	régler *to regulate, to settle*	-émer	écrémer *to skim*	-éser	léser *to injure*
-écher	lécher *to lick*	-égner	régner *to reign*	-éner	hydrgéner *to hydrogenate*	-éter	compléter *to complete*
-éder	posséder *to own*	-égrer	intégrer *to integrate*	-équer	hypothéquer *to mortgage*	-étrer	chronométrer *to time*

$$é \rightarrow è$$

<table>
<tr><td colspan="2">espérer → espè
(to hope)</td><td colspan="2">considérer → considèr
(to consider)</td></tr>
<tr><td>singular</td><td>plural</td><td>singular</td><td>plural</td></tr>
<tr><td>j'espèr -e</td><td>nous esper -ons</td><td>je considèr -e</td><td>nous considér -ons</td></tr>
<tr><td>tu espèr -es</td><td>vous esper -ez</td><td>tu considèr -es</td><td>vous considér -ez</td></tr>
<tr><td>il/elle/on espèr -e</td><td>ils/elles espèr -ent</td><td>il/elle/on considèr -e</td><td>ils/elles considèr -ent</td></tr>
</table>

Other verbs like **espérer** and **considérer** follow.

exagérer	posséder	préférer	répéter	suggérer
to exaggerate	*to possess*	*to prefer*	*to repeat*	*to suggest*

6-2a-5 For present tense regular verbs ending in **-ir,** drop the **-ir** and add the following endings.

finir singular subject	stem + ending		(to finish) plural subject	stem + ending	
je	fin	-is	nous	fin	-issons
tu	fin	-is	vous	fin	-issez
il/elle/on	fin	-it	ils/elles	fin	-issent

finir *to finish*	choisir *to choose*	applaudir *to clap*	remplir *to fill* *to refill*
bâtir *to build*	réunir *to bring together*	réfléchir *to consider*	réussir *to succeed*
grandir *to grow*	nourrir *to feed*	obéir *to obey*	punir *to punish*

All color-related verbs belong to the group of **finir** and follow its conjugation: **jaunir** *(to become yellow),* **noircir** *(to become black),* **blanchir** *(to become white),* **rougir** *(to blush),* **verdir** *(to become green),* **bleuir** *(to become blue).*

6-2a-6 Present tense of irregular verbs ending in **-ir**

✔ **Venir** and **tenir** change e → ie, in all but the first- and second-person plural forms. The following endings are then added.

venir singular subject	stem + ending		(to come) plural subject	stem + ending	
je	vien	-s	nous	ven	-ons
tu	vien	-s	vous	ven	-ez
il/elle/on	vien	-t	ils/elles	vien	-nent
tenir			*(to hold)*		
je	tien	-s	nous	ten	-ons
tu	tien	-s	vous	ten	-ez
il/elle/on	tien	-t	ils/elles	tien	-nent

Other verbs like **venir** follow.

s'abstenir *to refrain*	appartenir *to belong*	contenir *to contain*	détenir *to detain*	devenir *to become*
entretenir *to maintain*	intervenir *to intervene*	maintenir *to maintain*	obtenir *to obtain*	parvenir *to reach, to succeed*
retenir *to retain*	revenir *to return*	soutenir *to support*	se souvenir *to remember*	tenir *to hold*

✔ Partir and the following verbs ending in -**ir** drop the -**ir** and the consonant that precedes it to form the stem of the singular forms. To form the plural, simply drop the -**ir**. Add the following endings to the stem.

partir
singular

(to leave)
plural

subject	stem + ending		subject	stem + ending	
je	**par**	-s	nous	**part**	-ons
tu	**par**	-s	vous	**part**	-ez
il/elle/on	**par**	-t	ils/elles	**part**	-ent

Other verbs like **partir** appear below.

départir *to assign*	dormir *to sleep*	mentir *to lie*	repartir *to leave again*	répartir *to distribute*
ressentir *to feel*	sentir *to feel* *to smell*	servir *to serve*	sortir *to go out*	

✔ **Offrir** and the following verbs ending in -**ir** drop the -**ir** and add the endings shown below.

offrir
singular

(to offer)
plural

subject	stem + ending		subject	stem + ending	
j'	**offr**	-e	nous	**offr**	-ons
tu	**offr**	-es	vous	**offr**	-ez
il/elle/on	**offr**	-e	ils/elles	**offr**	-ent

accueillir	courir	couvrir	cueillir	découvrir
to welcome	*to run*	*to cover*	*to pick*	*to discover*
ouvrir	recouvrir	recueillir	souffrir	
to open	*to cover up*	*to gather*	*to suffer*	

✔ The **-our** in **mourir** *(to die)* changes to **-eur** in all but the first- and second-person plural forms.

singular	plural
je **meur -s**	nous **mour -ons**
tu **meur -s**	vous **mour -ez**
il/elle/on **meur -t**	ils/elles **meur -ent**

6-2a-7 Present tense of verbs ending in **-oir**

avoir (*to have*)

singular	plural
j'**ai**	nous **avons**
tu **as**	vous **avez**
il/elle/on **a**	ils/elles **ont**

✔ **Recevoir** and the following verbs share the same pattern.

recevoir (*to receive*)

singular subject	stem + ending		plural subject	stem + ending	
je	re	-çois	nous	recev	-ons
tu	re	-çois	vous	recev	-ez
il/elle/on	re	-çoit	ils/elles	re	-çoivent

apercevoir	concevoir	décevoir	percevoir
to notice	*to conceive*	*to deceive, to disappoint*	*to perceive*

voir *(to see)*

singular	plural
je vois	nous voyons
tu vois	vous voyez
il/elle/on voit	ils/elles voient

vouloir *(to want)*

singular	plural
je veux	nous voulons
tu veux	vous voulez
il/elle/on veut	ils/elles veulent

pouvoir *(to be able)*

singular	plural
je peux	nous pouvons
tu peux	vous pouvez
il/elle/on peut	ils/elles peuvent

devoir *(to have, to owe)*

singular	plural
je dois	nous devons
tu dois	vous devez
il/elle/on doit	ils/elles doivent

✔ The verbs **falloir, valoir (mieux),** and **pleuvoir** are conjugated only in the impersonal **il** form.

il faut   **il** vaut mieux   **il** pleut

Il faut que nous parlions français.   **Il pleut** à Paris.
We must speak French.   *It is raining in Paris.*

Il vaut mieux que tu écoutes attentivement.
It would be better if you listened carefully.

6-2a-8 Regular present tense verbs ending in **-re** drop the -re and add the endings shown.

perdre singular subject	stem + ending		plural subject	stem + ending
je	**perd**	-s	nous	**perd** -ons
tu	**perd**	-s	vous	**perd** -ez
il/elle/on	**perd**	-	ils/elles	**perd** -ent

(to lose)

attendre	confondre	entendre	rendre	répondre	vendre
to wait for	*to confuse*	*to hear*	*to return*	*to answer*	*to sell*

6-2a-9 The present tense of irregular verbs ending in **-re**

être *(to be)*

singular	plural
je suis	nous sommes
tu es	vous êtes
il/elle/on est	ils/elles sont

✔ **Connaître** and the verbs below drop the suffix **-ître** and add the endings shown.

The third-person singular takes a circumflex accent mark on the **î**.

connaître		*(to know)*	
singular subject	**stem + ending**	**plural subject**	**stem + ending**
je	connais	nous	connaissons
tu	connais	vous	connaissez
il/elle/on	connaît	ils/elles	connaissent

apparaître	disparaître	méconnaître	naître	paraître
to appear	*to disappear*	*to be unaware of*	*to be born*	*to appear, to seem*

✔ **Lire, élire,** and **relire** drop the suffix **-re** and add the following endings.

lire			*(to read)*		
singular subject	**stem**	**+ ending**	**plural subject**	**stem**	**+ ending**
je	li	-s	nous	li	-sons
tu	li	-s	vous	li	-sez
il/elle/on	li	-t	ils/elles	li	-sent

relire	élire	réélire
to reread	*to elect, to choose*	*to re-elect, to choose again*

✔ **Dire, contredire, interdire, prédire,** and **redire** drop the suffix **-re** and add the following endings.

dire			*(to say)*		
singular subject	**stem**	**+ ending**	**plural subject**	**stem**	**+ ending**
je	di	-s	nous	di	-sons
tu	di	-s	vous	di	-tes
il/elle/on	di	-t	ils/elles	di	-sent

contredire	interdire	prédire	redire
to contradict	*to forbid*	*to predict*	*to repeat, to say again*

✔ **Maudire** *(to curse)* follows the pattern of **finir.**

singular	plural
je **maud -is**	nous **maud -issons**
tu **maud -is**	vous **maud -issez**
il/elle/on **maud -it**	ils/elles **maud -issent**

✔ To conjugate **écrire**, drop the suffix **-re** and add the following endings. For **suivre** and **vivre** drop **-vre.**

écrire *(to write)*

singular subject	stem + ending		plural subject	stem + ending	
j'	écri	-s	nous	écri	-vons
tu	écri	-s	vous	écri	-vez
il/elle/on	écri	-t	ils/elles	écri	-vent

décrire	inscrire	récrire	transcrire	vivre
to describe	*to inscribe*	*to rewrite*	*to transcribe*	*to live*

suivre *(to follow)*

singular subject	stem + ending		plural subject	stem + ending	
je	sui	-s	nous	sui	-vons
tu	sui	-s	vous	sui	-vez
il/elle/on	sui	-t	ils/elles	sui	-vent

✔ **faire** *(to make, do)*

singular	plural
je fais	nous faisons
tu fais	vous faites
il/elle/on fait	ils/elles font

To conjugate **contrefaire**, drop **faire** and add the conjugations of **faire.**

contrefaire *(to imitate, to counterfeit)*

singular	plural
je contre**fais**	nous contrefais**ons**
tu contre**fais**	vous contre**faites**
il/elle/on contre**fait**	ils/elles contre**font**

défaire	refaire	satisfaire
to dismantle	*to do again*	*to satisfy*

✔ To conjugate the singular forms of **prendre,** drop the suffix **-re.** For the plural forms, drop the suffix **-ndre** and add the following endings.

prendre		*(to take)*		
singular		plural		
subject	stem + ending	subject	stem	+ ending
je	**prend** -s	nous	**pre**	-nons
tu	**prend** -s	vous	**pre**	-nez
il/elle/on	**prend** -	ils/elles	**pre**	-nnent

apprendre	comprendre	entreprendre	reprendre	surprendre
to learn	*to understand*	*to undertake*	*to resume*	*to surprise*

6-2a-10 Some irregular verbs ending in **-re** or **-ir** are conjugated like regular **-re** verbs except for the third-person singular form, which adds **-t** to the stem.

courir		*(to run)*		
singular		plural		
subject	stem + ending	subject	stem	+ ending
je	**cour** -s	nous	**cour**	-ons
tu	**cour** -s	vous	**cour**	-ez
il/elle/on	**cour** -t	ils/elles	**cour**	-ent

corrompre	interrompre	parcourir	rire	rompre	sourire
to corrupt	*to interrupt*	*to cover distance*	*to laugh*	*to break*	*to smile*

6-2a-11 Irregular verbs that end in **-re** and contain double consonants drop the ending plus one of the double consonants. You then add the **-re** endings for the singular form. For the plural forms, retain the double consonants and add the **-re** endings.

battre singular subject	stem + ending		*(to beat)* plural subject	stem + ending	
je	**bat**	-s	nous	**batt**	-ons
tu	**bat**	-s	vous	**batt**	-ez
il/elle/on	**bat**	-	ils/elles	**batt**	-ent

admettre *to admit*	combattre *to fight*	mettre *to put, to set, to place*	permettre *to permit*
promettre *to promise*	soumettre *to submit*	transmettre *to transmit*	

6-3 Present participles *express present action.*

✔ Present participles are formed by dropping the **-ons** ending of the first-person plural form of the present indicative and adding **-ant.**   parl**ons** → parl**ant**

✔ The English equivalent is the **-ing** form.

Exceptions are   avoir → ayant
                 être   → étant
                 savoir → sachant

However, to express ongoing actions in present time, French generally prefers the use of the present tense or the expression **être en train de** . . . rather than the use of the present participle.

Qu'est-ce que tu fais?   Je mange. *or* Je suis en train de manger.
What are you doing?   *I'm eating.*

✔ The **present participle** can be used to express action occurring simultaneously with the main verb.

Etant fatiguée elle conduisait dangereusement.
Because she was tired, she drove dangerously.

✔ As an adjective, the present participle indicates a distinctive quality, agreeing in gender and number with the noun it modifies.

L'histoire de Dalibá est **déchirante.**
Daliba's story is heart-breaking.

✔ The present participle is often used as a verb.

Déchirant le silence de la nuit, la femme criait angoissée.
Breaking the silence of the night, the woman screamed in anguish.

6-4 **Gerunds** *are formed with the preposition* **en** *and* **the present participle.**

✔ Gerunds refer to a verb and have the same subject as the verb. The gerund's action occurs at the same time as the action of the verb. To reinforce the idea of simultaneity, you can use **tout en**.

Tout en pleurant la mort de son chien elle cherchait un autre mascotte.
While mourning her dog's death, she looked for another pet.

✔ **Tout en** can also express contradiction.

Les enfants refusaient d'aller au lit, **tout en** ayant sommeil.
The children refused to go to bed, even though they were sleepy.

✔ In general, the present participle expresses time.

J'aime écrire **en écoutant** de la musique classique. (*when?* pendant que j'écoute...)
I like to write while listening to classical music.

✔ Present participles can also express the reason why something occurs.

C'est **en jouant** trop que Pierre s'est ruiné. (*why?* ... parce qu'il jouait...)
Pierre was ruined by too much gambling.

✔ Present participles can express the manner in which something occurred.

Elle a quitté la salle **en pleurant**. *(how?* ... en pleurant.)
She left the room crying.

✔ Present participles can express a condition.

En travaillant dur vous aurez de bonnes notes. (*If* ... si vous travaillez...)
By working hard, you will get good grades.

✔ When the present participle is introduced by the prepositon **en** or another preposition with the same meaning as **en,** it has the same meaning as *-ing* in English.

Je me suis endormi **en** conduissant ma voiture.
I fell asleep while driving my car.

C'est **en** étudiant tous les jours que tu réussiras.
It is by studying every day that you will succeed.

✔ With other prepositions, use the infinitive instead of the present participle.

Réfléchissez **avant** de **répondre.**
Think before answering.

✔ Do not use the present participle after the preposition **après,** which requires the perfect infinitive **avoir** or **être,** and the past participle.

Après avoir dit ça, elle est partie.
After saying that, she left.

6-5 The passé simple *is a literary tense that presents a completed action in the past. In spoken and informal written French, the passé composé is used.*

✔ As a literary tense, the **passé simple** is almost always used in the third-person singular.

Honte de boire! **acheva** le buveur qui **s'enferma** définitivement dans le silence.
Ashamed of drinking! The tippler brought his speech to an end, and shut himself up in an impregnable silence.

Antoine de Saint-Exupéry, *Le Petit Prince*

✔ The action of the **passé simple** has no contact with the present.

✔ The action of verbs in the **passé simple** is considered as something distant.

6-5a The passé simple of regular verbs ending in **-er** drops the -er and adds the following endings

parler	*(to talk)*
singular	**plural**
je **parl -ai**	nous **parl -âmes**
tu **parl -as**	vous **parl -âtes**
il/elle/on **parl -a**	ils/elles **parl -èrent**

6-5b The passé simple of regular verbs ending in **-ir** drops the -ir and adds the following endings:

finir	*(to finish)*
singular	**plural**
je **fin -is**	nous **fin -îmes**
tu **fin -is**	vous **fin -îtes**
il/elle/on **fin -it**	ils/elles **fin -irent**

6-5c The passé simple of regular verbs ending in **-re** drops the -re and adds the following endings.

rendre	*(to give back, to return something)*
singular	**plural**
je **rend -is**	nous **rend -îmes**
tu **rend -is**	vous **rend -îtes**
il/elle/on **rend -it**	ils/elles **rend -irent**

6-5d The passé simple of irregular verbs is usually formed with the past participle.

✔ Past participles ending in *u*

avoir   *(to have)*

singular	plural
j' e-**us**	nous e-**ûmes**
tu e-**us**	vous e-**ûtes**
il/elle/on e-**ut**	ils/elles e-**urent**

boire: *to drink*	bu	→	je bus	connaître: *to know*	connu →	je connus
courir: *to run*	couru	→	je courus	devoir: *to have, to owe*	dû →	je dus
falloir: *to be necessary*	fallu	→	il fallut	lire: *to read*	lu →	je lus
paraître: *to seem*	paru	→	je parus	plaire: *to please*	plu →	je plus
pleuvoir: *to rain*	plu	→	il plut	pouvoir: *to be able*	pu →	je pus
recevoir: *to receive*	reçu	→	je reçus	savoir: *to know*	su →	je sus
se taire: *to be silent*	tu	→	je me tus	valoir: *to be worth*	valu →	je valus
vivre: *to live*	vécu	→	je vécus	vouloir: *to want*	voulu →	je voulus

✔ Past participles ending in *i*

dire *(to say)*

singular	plural
je **di** -s	nous **d** -**îmes**
tu **di** -s	vous **d** -**îtes**
il/elle/on **di** -t	ils/elles **d** -**irent**

---

s'asseoir: assis → je m'assis   dormir: dormi → je dormis   mettre: mis → je mis
to sit down   *to sleep*   *to put*

✔ The **passé simple** of **tenir, venir,** and their compounds.

tenir *(to hold)*

singular	**plural**
je tins	nous tînmes
tu tins	vous tîntes
il/elle/on tint	ils/elles tinrent

venir	→	vins	revenir	→	revins
to come			*to return*		

✔ The following verbs do not form their passé simple from the past participle.

être	→	je fus	écrire	→	j' écrivis	faire	→	je fis
mourir	→	je mourus	naître	→	je naquis	voir	→	je vis

6-6 The passé récent *expresses an action completed in the near past.*

✔ The **passé récent** is formed with the present tense of **venir + de + infinitive.**

Je **viens de finir** mon nouveau roman.
I have just finished my new novel.

✔ Used in the non-immediate past, **venir** is conjugated in the imperfect.

Je **venais** d'arriver des vacances quand j'ai reçu la lettre d'acceptation à l'université.
I had just come back from vacation when I received an acceptance letter from the university.

6-7 The passé composé *expresses fully-completed actions that occurred in a specific time in the past.*

✔ The **passé composé** is a compound tense formed as follows.

present tense of the auxiliary verb *avoir* (p. 71) **or** *être* (p. 73) **+ past participle** (p. 81).

j'ai chanté	je suis venu	j'ai perdu
I sang	*I came*	*I lost*

Je **suis allé** à Avignon l'été dernier.
I went to Avignon last summer.

J'ai **perdu** mon portefeuille.
I lost my wallet.

J'ai **fini** mes devoirs.
I finished my homework.

✔ In negative sentences, **ne** (**n'**) comes before the auxiliary verb and **pas** comes after it.

Je **ne** suis **pas** allé au cinéma.
I didn't go to the movies.

Je **n' ai** pas **fini** de manger.
I haven't finished eating.

✔ Most French verbs form the passé composé with the present tense of the auxiliary verb **avoir** and **the past participle**.

6-7a Uses of the passé composé

✔ The **passé composé** expresses a completed action in the past.

Je **suis allé** au Chili l'année dernière.
I went to Chile last year.

J'ai fait mes devoirs en dix minutes.
I finished my homework in ten minutes.

✔ Use the **passé composé** to indicate a series of actions or events completed in the past.

Je **me suis levé** vers six heures, j'**ai pris** mon petit déjeuner et j'**ai quitté** la maison vers huit heures trente.
I got up around six, ate my breakfast, and left around eight-thirty.

✔ The passé composé is used to express repeated past actions if they are considered as a complete unit or if the end is stressed.

J'ai vu Jean quatre fois l'année dernière.
I saw Jean four times last year.

6-8 The past participle *is the form of the verb that implies completion. That is, the action described by the verb is completed at some point in time.*

6-8a Past participle endings of regular verbs are formed by replacing the infinitive endings with the past participle endings.

er	→ é	ir	→ i	re	→ u
chanter	→ chanté	finir	→ fini	perdre	→ perdu
to sing		*to finish*		*to lose*	

6-8b Some past participle endings of irregular verbs follow.

apprendre *to learn*	→	appris	avoir *to have*	→	eu	battre *to hit,* *to beat*	→	battu
boire *to drink*	→	bu	comprendre *to understand*	→	compris	conduire *to drive*	→	conduit
connaître *to know*	→	connu	courir *to run*	→	couru	couvrir *to cover*	→	couvert
croir *to believe*	→	cru	devoi *to have to,* *to owe*	→	dû	dire *to say*	→	dit
écrire *to write*	→	écrit	être *to be*	→	été	faire *to do,* *to make*	→	fait
falloir *to be necessary*	→	fallu	lire *to read*	→	lu	mettre *to put*	→	mis
mourir *to die*	→	mort	naître *to be born*	→	né	ouvrir *to open*	→	ouvert
plaire *to please*	→	plu	pleuvoir *to rain*	→	plu	prendre *to take*	→	pris
recevoir *to receive*	→	reçu	rire *to laugh*	→	ri	souffrir *to suffer*	→	souffert
venir *to come*	→	venu	vivre *to live*	→	vécu	voir *to see*	→	vu

6-8b-1 Agreement of the past participle

✔ The past participle of verbs conjugated with the auxiliary **avoir** agrees in gender and number with the direct object pronoun only when the latter is placed in front of the verb.

La lettre?   Je l'ai déjà écrite.
The letter?   *I already wrote it.*

✔ There is no agreement with **y, dont,** or **en.**

De belles statues?   Il en a **vu.**
Beautiful statues?   *He has seen some.*

✔ When the auxilary verb is **être,** the past participle agrees in gender and number with the subject.

Elle est arrivée à Paris vers minuit.
She arrived in Paris around midnight.

✔ The past participle of the reflexive and reciprocal verbs agrees in gender and number with the preceding direct object.

Marie s'est lavée.
Marie washed herself.

✔ When the direct object follows the verb, there is no agreement.

Marie s'est lavé **les cheveux.**
Marie washed her hair.

Note: The verbs **monter, descendre, sortir, rentrer, retourner** and **passer** use **avoir** when they have a direct object.

J'ai descendu **le livre de l'étagère.**
I took the book down from the shelf.

J'ai sorti **ma voiture** du garage.
I took my car out of the garage.

Nous avons passé **de bonnes vacances.**
We had a good vacation.

6-8c Verbs that form the passé composé with être appear below.

aller *(to go)*	Je **suis allé** à la gare.
	I went to the train station.
apparaître *(to appear)*	Le train **est apparu.**
	The train appeared.
arriver *(to arrive)*	Il **est arrivé** à minuit pile.
	It arrived at midnight sharp.
descendre *(to go down)*	Elle **est descendue** lentement de la voiture.
	She climbed down very slowly from the car.
venir *(to come)*	Elle **est venue** vers moi,
	She came towards me,
entrer *(to enter)*	elle **est entrée** dans ma vie.
	and she entered my life.
naître *(to be born)*	Cette nuit-là un amour **est né.**
	That night a love was born.
mourir *(to die)*	Mon passé **est mort** dans ses bras.
	My past died in her arms.
partir *(to leave)*	Nous **sommes partis** vers l'avenir.
	We left for the future.
rester *(to stay)*	La gare **est restée** seule.
	The station stayed alone.
retourner *(to return)*	Nous ne **sommes** jamais **retournés** à cette gare,
	We never returned to that station,
tomber *(to fall)*	où, à minuit pile nous **sommes tombés** amoureux.
	where, at midnight sharp we fell in love.
Monter *(to climb)*, sortir *(to go out)*?	C'est une autre histoire.
	That's another story.

Gustavo Gac-Artigas

All the above verbs and their compounds, as well as **passer, décéder, devenir, revenir,** and all the reflexive verbs, use **être** as auxilary verb for the **passé composé**.

6-9 The **imperfect tense** *is a tense used to designate a past action or condition that is incomplete, continuous, or coincides with another action.*

✔ The imperfect is formed by dropping the **-ons** from the first-person plural of the present indicative and adding the endings of the imperfect.

| chanter *(to sing)* | | finir *(to finish)* | | perdre *(to lose)* | |
chant ons → chant		finiss ons → finiss		perd ons → perd	
subject	stem + ending	subject	stem + ending	subject	stem+ ending
je	chant -ais	je	finiss -ais	je	perd -ais
tu	chant -ais	tu	finiss -ais	tu	perd -ais
il/elle/on	chant -ait	il/elle/on	finiss -ait	il/elle/on	perd -ait
nous	chant -ions	nous	finiss -ions	nous	perd -ions
vous	chant -iez	vous	finiss -iez	vous	perd -iez
ils/elles	chant -aient	il/elles	finiss -aient	il/elles	perd -aient

6-9a The imperfect of **avoir** and **être**

✔ The only irregular verbs in the imperfect are **avoir** and **être**.

avoir *(to have)*		être *(to be)*	
singular	**plural**	**singular**	**plural**
j'avais	nous avions	j'étais	nous étions
tu avais	vous aviez	tu étais	vous étiez
il/elle/on avait	ils/elles avaient	il/elle/on était	ils/elles étaient

6-9b Verbs with spelling changes in the first and second person plurals of the imperfect.

| -cer (c → ç) | | -ger (ge → gi) | |
commencer *(to begin)*		manger *(to eat)*	
subject	stem + ending	subject	stem + ending
je	commen -çais	je	man -geais
tu	commen -çais	tu	man -geais
il/elle/on	commen -çait	il/elle/on	man -geait
nous	commen -cions *	nous	man -gions *
vous	commen -ciez *	vous	man -giez*
ils/elles	commen -çaient	ils/elles	man -geaient

*c before **i** or **e** sounds like **s**; therefore, the cedilla is not needed. **g** before **i** or **e** sounds like a soft **g**; therefore, the **e** is not needed.

6-9c Uses of the imperfect

✔ In English the imperfect is equivalent to **was doing, used to do** or **did**, or **would + infinitive**.

✔ The imperfect expresses habitual or repeated actions in the past. There is no clear moment when these actions begin or end.

Quand nous **étions** petits nous passions toujours nos vacances à la mer.
When we were children we always went on vacation to the sea.

✔ The imperfect expresses a wish, suggestion, or supposition in **si** clauses.

Et **si** vous **partiez** tout de suite?
And if you left immediately?

✔ The imperfect is used with **pendant** to describe simultaneous actions in the past.

Elle lisait **pendant** que j'écrivais.
She read while I was writing.

✔ Use the imperfect to tell time and express age in the past.

Il **était** huit heures quand le drame a eu lieu.
It was eight o'clock when the drama occurred.

Melina **avait** cinq ans quand elle a commencé à lire toute seule.
Melina was five when she started to read by herself.

✔ The imperfect is used in indirect discourse when the verb of the main clause is in the past.

Le Prophète a dit qu'il **était** destiné à mourir.
The prophet said that he was destined to die.

✔ Use the imperfect to begin a story.

Il **était** une fois un grand loup plein de bonté et une petite fille méchante...
Once upon a time there was a big kind, wolf and a mean little girl...

6-9d Imperfect vs. passé composé

The **passé composé** and **imperfect** tenses are two ways of expressing past actions and events, but each tense is used within a specific context and follows specific criteria. Sometimes the choice of one or the other tense depends on the way the speaker views the action or event. In general, the passé composé is associated with actions completed in the past while the imperfect is used to describe routine actions and states of being.

Imperfect

✔ If telling a story in the past:

The **imperfect** provides the description of the scenario. External conditions such as time, date, weather, etc. are usually expressed with the imperfect.

Il était dix heures du matin d'un beau jour de printemps. **Il faisait** chaud et le soleil **brillait** au milieu du ciel. Marie et les enfants **se promenaient** dans le parc.
It was ten o'clock in the morning on a beautiful summer day. It was hot, and the sun was shining in the center of the sky. Marie and the children were strolling in the park.

✔ The imperfect is used to describe the characters' appearance.

Elle **était** jeune et belle. Elle **portait** une blouse blanche et une jupe rose. Les enfants, qui **avaient** quatre et cinq ans...
She was young and pretty. She was wearing a white blouse with a pink skirt. The children, who were four and five years old...

✔ The imperfect is used to describe background activities such as what was going on, or what people were doing.

...**jouaient** auprès d'un arbre pendant que Marie **lisait** un livre sur un banc....
...were playing happily near a tree while Marie was reading a book on a bench.

Passé composé

The **passé composé** provides the actions that develop the story line. These actions must have been completed in the past and be specific, not continuous or descriptive.

Soudain, un des enfants **a commencé** à crier. Marie **a couru** pour voir ce qui se passait. Quand elle **est arrivée** auprès des enfants, elle **a vu** que le plus petit, Julien, pleurait accroché à la branche d'un arbre.
Suddenly, one of the kids started screaming. Marie ran to find out what was going on. When she arrived at the place where the kids were playing, she saw that the youngest one, Julien, was hanging from a tree branch, crying.

✔ In some situations, either the passé composé or the imperfect may be used, depending on how the speaker sees the action or series of actions:

Imperfect	Passé composé
✔ habitual or repetitive action	✔ action seen as a specific completed unit

1) Jeanne **travaillait** toute la journée.
Jeanne used to work all day long.

2) En été nous **allions** à la plage tous les jours.
We used to go to the beach every day during the summer.

3) Quand j'**étais** étudiante à la fac, tous les jours, je **prenais** mes livres et je **partais** pour l'université.
When I was a college student, every day I used to get my books and leave for school.

1) Françoise **a travaillé** toute la journée.
Françoise worked all day long.

2) En été nous **sommes allés** à la plage tous les jours.
In summer we went to the beach every day.

3) Ce matin j'**ai pris** mes livres et je **suis parti** pour la fac.
This morning I got my books and left for school.

✔ To describe a physical or mental condition or state of mind, use the guidelines that follow.

Imperfect	Passé composé

✔ Use the imperfect to describe a physical or mental condition or state of mind.

Hier soir j'**avais** de la fièvre.
Last night I had a fever.

Jean **se sentait** très triste.
Jean felt very sad.

✔ When a physical or mental condition or state of mind is viewed as having ended, use the **passé composé.**

Hier soir j'**ai eu** de la fièvre toute la nuit.
I had a fever all night long last night.

Jean **s'est senti** très triste.
Jean felt very sad. (He doesn't feel sad anymore.)

✔ For **indirect discourse** relating oral statements without quoting them directly, use the following guidelines:

Imperfect	Passé composé

✔ Use the imperfect for the conversation that's being reported indirectly.

Monsieur Durand a dit qu'il **était** fatigué.
Mr. Durand said he was tired.

Le directeur a dit qu'il n'**était** pas nécessaire d'arriver si tôt.
The director said that it was not necessary to arrive so early.

✔ Use the **passé composé** for the relating verb.

Monsieur Durand **a dit** qu'il était fatigué.
Mr. Durand said he was tired.

Le directeur **a dit** qu'il n'était pas nécessaire d'arriver si tôt.
The director said that it was not necessary to arrive so early.

Some other verbs used in indirect discourse are **confirmer** (*to confirm*), **répondre** (*to answer*), and **demander** (*to ask*).

✔ **Parallel actions** using the imperfect and the **passé composé**

Imperfect	Passé composé
✔ The imperfect describes simultaneous actions seen as ongoing process in the past.	✔ The **passé composé** describes completed actions started at the same time in the past.
Pendant que Charles **lisait** un roman, Pierre **écrivait** une lettre. *While Charles was reading a novel, Pierre was writing a letter and we were watching TV.*	Pendant que Charles **a lu** un roman, Pierre **a écrit** une lettre et nous **avons regardé** la télé. *While Charles read a novel, Pierre wrote a letter and we watched TV.*

Imperfect	Passé composé
✔ When action in progress is interrupted by another action, the imperfect is used to describe the action in progress.	✔ The action that interrupts the action that was in progress takes the **passé composé**.
Quand nous **marchions** dans la rue, Jean s'est approché de nous. *When we were walking down the street, Jean approached us.*	Quand nous marchions dans la rue, Jean **s'est approché** de nous. *When we were walking down the street, Jean approached us.*
✔ When action in progress is contrasted to a completed action, the imperfect is used for the action in progress.	✔ The **passé composé** is used for the completed action that took place against the background of the ongoing action.
Pendant que Charles **lisait**, Jean a fait ses devoirs. *Jean finished his homework while Charles was reading.*	Pendant que Charles lisait, Jean **a fait** ses devoirs. *Jean finished his homework while Charles was reading.*

6-10 The pluperfect *is used to express or describe an action completed prior to another action in the past. In English, the pluperfect is conjugated with* **had** *plus the* **past participle** *of the verb.*

✔ French forms the pluperfect with the imperfect of **être** or **avoir** (p. 84) plus the past participle (p. 81).

singular	plural	singular	plural
j'avais parlé	nous avions parlé	j'étais parti(e)	nous étions parti(e)s
tu avais parlé	vous aviez parlé	tu étais parti(e)	vous étiez parti(e)s
il/elle/on avait parlé	ils/elles avaient parlé	il/elle/on était parti(e)	ils/elles étaient parti(e)s

Quand tu as téléphoné, Pierre **était** déjà **parti**.
Pierre had already left when you called.

Nous **avions fini** d'étudier quand le professeur est arrivé.
We had (already) finished studying when the professor arrived.

✔ The pluperfect is used to express an action completed prior to another action in the past.

Hier nous sommes allés au restaurant dont tu nous **avais** parlé la semaine dernière.
Yesterday we went to the restaurant you told us about last week.

✔ To describe a condition or a state existing in the past prior to another condition or state, use the pluperfect.

Il **était devenu** célèbre même avant la publication de son deuxième roman.
He had become famous even before the publishing of his second novel.

✔ Use the pluperfect with the preposition **si** to express a hypothetical past event.

Si tu **étais allé** chez le médecin hier, tu te sentirais mieux aujourd'hui.
If you had gone to the doctor yesterday, you would feel better today.

6-11 The future tense *expresses actions that have not yet occurred.*

✔ A future action in English is expressed with **will** or **shall** plus a **verb**.

Je **finirai** mes études dans trois ans.
I will finish my studies in three years.

✔ The future tense in French is formed by adding the appropriate endings to the infinitive.

chanter *(to sing)*	finir *(to finish)*	perdre *(to lose)*
chanter-	finir-	perdr-

✔ If the infinitive ends in -re, drop the -e before adding the endings, except for **faire**.

subject	stem + ending	subject	stem + ending	subject	stem + ending
je	chanter -ai	je	finir -ai	je	perdr -ai
tu	chanter -as	tu	finir -as	tu	perdr -as
il/elle/on	chanter -a	il/elle/on	finir -a	il/elle/on	perdr -a
nous	chanter -ons	nous	finir -ons	nous	perdr -ons
vous	chanter -ez	vous	finir -ez	vous	perdr -ez
ils/elles	chanter -ont	ils/elles	finir -ont	ils/elles	perdr -ont

✔ Unlike the -re verbs above, **faire** changes to **fer-**; then the endings are added.

faire *(to make, to do)*

singular		plural	
je	fer -ai	nous	fer -ons
tu	fer -as	vous	fer -ez
il/elle/on	fer -a	il/elles/on	fer -ont

✔ Verbs with stem changes in the present have the same changes in the future.

6-11a Accent mark change: e → è

✔ Add an accent grave to all forms.

amener → amèner
(to bring along)

acheter → achèter
(to buy)

subject	stem + ending	subject	stem + ending
j'	amèner -ai	j'	achèter -ai
tu	amèner -as	tu	achèter -as
il/elle/on	amèner -a	il/elle/on	achèter -a
nous	amèner -ons	nous	achèter -ons
vous	amèner -ez	vous	achèter -ez
ils/elles	amèner -ont	ils/elles	achèter -ont

amener *(to bring along)*

acheter *(to buy)*

6-11b Letter changes

✔ Some regular -er verbs double the consonant before the verb ending in all persons.

appeler → appell-
(to call)

jeter → jett-
(to throw)

subject	stem + ending		subject	stem + ending	
j'	appeller	-ai	je	jetter	-ai
tu	appeller	-as	tu	jetter	-as
il/elle/on	appeller	-a	il/elle/on	jetter	-a
nous	appeller	-ons	nous	jetter	-ons
vous	appeller	-ez	vous	jetter	-ez
ils/elles	appeller	-ont	ils/elles	jetter	-ont

exceptions: acheter and geler take an accent mark change: e → è (See page 90).

✔ The y in some verbs changes to i in all forms.

essayer → essaier
(to try)

payer→ paier
(to pay)

subject	stem + ending		subject	stem + ending	
j'	essaier	-ai	je	paier	-ai
tu	essaier	-as	tu	paier	-as
il/elle/on	essaier	-a	il/elle/on	paier	-a
nous	essaier	-ons	nous	paier	-ons
vous	essaier	-ez	vous	paier	-ez
ils/elles	essaier	-ont	ils/elles	paier	-ont

6-11c Verbs with irregular stems in the future

acquérir *to acquire*	→ acquerr-	aller *to go*	→ ir-	avoir *to have*	→ aur-
conquérir *to conquer*	→ conquerr-	courir *to run*	→ courr-	devoir *to have, to owe*	→ devr-
envoyer *to send*	→ enverr-	être *to be*	→ ser-	falloir *to be necessary*	→ faudr-
faire *to do, to make*	→ fer-	mourir *to die*	→ mourr-	obtenir *to obtain*	→ obtiendr-
pleuvoir *to rain*	→ pleuvr-	pouvoir *to be able*	→ pourr-	recevoir *to receive*	→ recevr-
savoir *to know*	→ saur-	tenir *to hold*	→ tiendr-	valoir *to be worth*	→ vaudr-
venir *to come*	→ viendr-	voir *to see*	→ verr-	vouloir *to want*	→ voudr-

✔ The future tense can express a future action leave that will take place soon or not for a while.

Il **pleuvra** ce soir.　　　　　　　　　Nous **partirons** en vacances l'été prochain.
It will rain tonight.　　　　　　　　　*We will go on vacation next summer.*

✔ Use the future tense instead of the imperative to soften a command.

Vous m'**apporterez** le rapport lundi prochain.
You will bring me the report next Monday.

✔ The future tense is always required after the conjunctions **quand, lorsque** (*when*), **dès que,**
aussitôt que (*as soon as*), **après que** (*after...*), and **tant que** (*as long as*) when a future idea is
implied. The action introduced by these expressions has not yet taken place.

Future + quand/lorsque/dès que/aussitôt que/après que/tant que + future

Je vous **téléphonerai** dès que j'**arriverai** chez moi.
I will call you (future) as soon as I get (present) home.

(Note that this use of the future in French differs from the English.)

Lorsque je **serai** à Paris, je **visiterai** le Louvre.
When I am in Paris, I will visit the Louvre.

Imperative + quand/lorsque/dès que/aussitôt que/après que/tant que, + future

Téléphonez-nous quand vous **aurez** le temps.
Call us when you have time.

6-12 The future perfect *is a compound tense used to express a future action will be completed after another action in the future has taken place.*

✔ The future perfect is formed with the future tense of the auxiliary verb and the past participle of the main verb.

> future of **avoir** or **être** + **participe passé** (See page 81.)
> *will have* + *past participle*

avoir		être	
j'aurai fini	nous aurons fini	je serai allé(e)	nous serons allé(e)s
tu auras fini	vous aurez fini	tu seras allé(e)	vous serez allé(e)s
il/elle/on aura fini	ils/elles auront fini	il/elle/on sera allé(e)	ils/elles seront allé(e)s

Je suis sûr que j'**aurai appris** le français avant d'aller à Paris.
I am sure that I will have learned French before going to Paris.

✔ When used alone, the future perfect expresses a completed action in a precise moment of the future. It is usually accompanied by a time expression.

Dans une semaine j'**aurai fini** mon roman.
I will have finished my novel in one week.

✔ The future perfect can express probability.

Jean n'est pas venu; **aura**-t-il **eu** un accident?
Jean didn't come; he probably had an accident.

✔ The future perfect is used after the conjunctions **quand, lorsque** (*when*), **dès que, aussitôt que** (*as soon as*), **après que** (*after*), and **tant que** (*as long as*), when a future action is implied but has not yet taken place.

Je passerai te voir **dès que** j'**aurai fini** le rapport.
I will come to see you as soon as I've finished the report.

Tant que je **n'aurai pas fini** le travail je ne serai pas tranquille.
As long as I haven't finished my work, I will not be at peace.

Partez **aussitôt que vous aurez** visité le musée.
Leave as soon as you've visited the museum.

6-13 The **near future** *is used to express actions or events that will occur in the near future.*

✔ The near future is formed with the present tense of **aller** plus the **infinitive**.

aller *(to go)* **+ partir** *(to leave, depart)*

singular subject		plural subject	
je	vais partir	nous	allons partir
tu	vas partir	vous	allez partir
il/elle/on	va partir	ils/elles	vont partir

Nous **allons partir** la semaine prochaine.
We are going to leave next week.

✔ The English equivalent is **to be going** + infinitive.

Allez-vous étudier plus tard?
Are you going to study later?

✔ The near future indicates certainty that an action will take place in a distant future.

Dans cinq ans **nous allons fêter** nos noces d'argent.
In five years we are going to celebrate our silver wedding anniversary.

6-13a Expressions of future time

✔ Expressions with **demain** *(tomorrow)*

demain matin	*tomorrow morning*
demain après-midi	*tomorrow afternoon*
demain soir	*tomorrow*

✔ Expressions with **prochain** *(next)*

lundi prochain	*next Monday*
la semaine prochaine	*next week*
le mois prochain	*next month*
l'année prochaine	*next year*
seasons: l'été prochain	*next summer*

6-13b Agreement between the tenses in the future

✔ Sentences conveying the idea of future include a main clause with a verb in the **future** and a dependent clause with a verb in the **present** or imperative.

Si vous me **donnez** la réponse je **partirai** heureuse.
If you give me the answer, I will leave happily.

Donnez-moi la réponse et je **partirai** heureuse.
Give me the answer and I will leave happily.

✔ To convey the idea of future within the framework of the past, use sentences with a main clause in the **future** or **imperative**, plus **quand/lorsque/dès que/aussitôt que/après que/tant que** and a dependent clause in the **future** or **future perfect**.

Je **partirai** quand vous me **donnerez** (m'**aurez donné**) la réponse.
I will leave when you've told me the answer.

Quand vous **finirez** (**aurez fini**) le livre, **rendez**-le à la bibliothèque.
When you've finished the book, return it to the library.

6-14 The conditional *is a mood expressing a hypothetical situation that may or may not take place, or that is subject to some condition introduced by a si clause before it can take place.*

Si j'étais à votre place, j'**étudierais** avant l'examen.
If I were you, I would study before the test.

Vous **auriez** de meilleurs résultats si vous étudiez tous les jours.
You would get better results if you studied every day.

✔ The conditional has two tenses, **present** and **past**.

6-14a The present conditional is formed by adding the endings below to the infinitive.

✔ The English equivalent is **would + verb.**

chanter (*to sing*)	**finir** (*to finish*)	**perdre** (*to lose*)
		perdre perdr

✔ If the infinitive ends in **-re,** drop the **-e** before adding the endings, except for **faire.**

chanter (*to sing*)   **finir** (*to finish*)   **perdre** (*to lose*)

perdre → perdr

subject	stem + ending	subject	stem + ending	subject	stem + ending
singular		**singular**		**singular**	
je	chanter -ais	je	finir -ais	je	perdr -ais
tu	chanter -ais	tu	finir -ais	tu	perdr -ais
il/elle/on	chanter -ait	il/elle/on	finir -ait	il/elle/on	perdr -ait
plural		**plural**		**plural**	
nous	chanter -ions	nous	finir -ions	nous	perdr -ions
vous	chanter -iez	vous	finir -iez	vous	perdr -iez
ils/elles	chanter -aient	ils/elles	finir -aient	ils/elles	perdr -aient

Faire is the exception to the rule stated above. **faire → fer.**

faire (*to make, do*)

singular		plural	
je	**fer ais**	nous	**fer ions**
tu	**fer ais**	vous	**fer iez**
il/elle/on	**fer ait**	ils/elles	**fer aient**

6-14a-1 Irregular verbs in the present conditional

✔ Use the same stems as the irregular verbs in future.

aller *to go*	→	ir	acquérir *to acquire*	→	acquerr	avoir *to have*	→	aur
conquérir *to conquer*	→	conquerr	courir *to run*	→	courr	devoir *to have, to owe*	→	devr
envoyer *to send*	→	enverr	être *to be*	→	ser	falloir *to be necessary*	→	faudr
faire *to do, to make*	→	fer	mourir *to die*	→	mourr	obtenir *to obtain*	→	obtiendr
pleuvoir *to rain*	→	pleuvr	pouvoir *to be able*	→	pourr	recevoir *to receive*	→	recevr
savoir *to know*	→	saur	tenir *to hold*	→	tiendr	valoir *to be worth*	→	vaudr
venir *to come*	→	viendr	voir *to see*	→	verr	vouloir *to want*	→	voudr

6-14b Uses of the conditional

✔ Use the present conditional to tell what would happen in the future with regard to an event in the past.

Hier on m'a dit que ma fille **serait** une grande pianiste.
Yesterday they told me that my daughter would be a great pianist.

✔ The conditional is also used to soften requests, statements, or commands.

✔ The conditional is usually used with **pouvoir, vouloir,** and **aimer.**

Pourriez-vous m'aider?   **Voudriez**-vous m'accompagner?
Could you help me?   *Would you accompany me?*

✔ Use the conditional to express a wish or a dream.

J'**aimerais** bien aller en vacances.
I would like to go on vacation.

✔ Use the conditional to express information that is not necessarily accurate.

Le témoin oculaire a dit qu'il y **aurait** au moins une trentaine de morts.
The eyewitness said that there would be at least thirty dead.

✔ The conditional can express an imaginary event.

Ils **marcheraient** la main dans la main vers l'avenir.
They would walk hand in hand toward the future.

✔ Use the conditional to express a possibility or supposition.

Va le voir aujourd'hui, demain ce **serait** trop tard.
Go see him today, tomorrow might be too late.

✔ The conditional is used in **si** clauses where the condition is expressed with the imperfect.

S'il n'était pas marié, je l'**épouserais**.
If he were not married, I would marry him.

6-14c The conditional perfect is used to express what would have occurred at a point in the past.

✔ The conditional perfect can be translated in English as **would have + past participle.**

✔ The conditional perfect is formed with the present conditional of the auxiliary verb (**avoir** or **être**) and the **past participle** of the verb (p. 81).

	conditional of avoir + past participle		conditional of être + past participle
singular		**singular**	
j'	aurais chanté	je	serais allé(e)
tu	aurais chanté	tu	serais allé(e)
il/elle/on	aurait chanté	il/elle/on	serait allé(e)
plural		**plural**	
nous	aurions chanté	nous	serions allé(e)s
vous	auriez chanté	vous	seriez allé(e)(s)
ils/elles	auraient chanté	ils/elles	seraient allé(e)s

Elle **serait allée** en France si elle avait eu le temps.
She would have gone to France if she had had the time.

✔ Use the conditional perfect to express regret or indignation.

J'**aurais** bien **fini** mes études, mais je n'ai pas pu.
I would have finished my studies, but I couldn't.

CHART 11	AGREEMENT BETWEEN THE TENSES IN HYPOTHETICAL SYSTEMS

CONDITION	RÉSULTAT
présent Si j'**ai** le temps... *If I have time...*	**futur** ...j'**irai** vous voir. *...I will come to see you.*
imparfait Si j'**avais** le temps... *If I had time...*	**conditionnel présent** ...j'**irais** vous voir. *...I would come to see you.*
plus-que-parfait Si j'**avais eu** le temps... *If I had had time...*	**conditionnel passé** ...je **serais allé** vous voir. *...I would have come to see you.*

6-15 The subjunctive *is an attitude the speaker has toward a fact or action. It primarily indicates that something is not a fact or that something might happen.*

✔ The subjunctive has four tenses.

present subjunctive	**que je chante**	*that I sing*
imperfect subjunctive	**que je chantasse**	*that I sang*
present perfect subjunctive	**que j'aie chanté**	*that I have sung*
pluperfect subjunctive	**que j'eusse chanté**	*that I had sung*

✔ The subjunctive is used to express an attitude, feelings, beliefs, or opinions about an idea or fact and to express statements or questions that reflect emotion, possibility, influence, nonexistence, or uncertainty.

✔ The subjunctive represents a contingent or hypothetical act or state, actions viewed subjectively, or subordinate statements.

✔ The subjunctive is usually subordinate to another dominating idea, or the independent clause, that contains the verb in the indicative mood.

✔ Dependent clauses contain the verb in the subjunctive which is often introduced by **que**.

✔ The subjunctive can also be used alone in idiomatic expressions.

Sauve qui peut!	Vive la République!	Soit!
Every man for himself!	*Long live the Republic!*	*So be it!*

✔ When preceded by **que**, the subjunctive is used as a command in the third-person singular or plural.

Que tout le monde **se taise!**
Everyone be quiet!

✔ There are four conditions that call for the use of the subjunctive.

volition	**emotion** and **feelings**	**unreality**	**doubt** and **denial**

6-16 Present subjunctive

✔ The subjunctive is formed with the stem of the third-person plural of the present indicative and the endings.

chanter (*to sing*)
chant ent → chant

finir (*to finish*)
finiss ent → finiss

perdre (*to lose*)
perd ent → perd

subject	stem + ending		subject	stem + ending		subject	stem + ending	
singular			**singular**			**singular**		
que je	chant	e	que je	finiss	e	que je	perd	e
que tu	chant	es	que tu	finiss	es	que tu	perd	es
qu'il/elle/on	chant	e	que il/elle/on	finiss	e	que il/elle/on	perd	e
plural			**plural**			**plural**		
que nous	chant	ions	que nous	finiss	ions	que nous	perd	ions
que vous	chant	iez	que vous	finiss	iez	que vous	perd	iez
qu'ils/elles	chant	ent	qu'ils/elles	finiss	ent	qu'ils/elles	perd	ent

✔ All the verbs except **être** and **avoir** have the same endings.

	avoir *(to have)*	**être** *(to be)*
	singular	**singular**
que	j'aie	que je sois
que	tu aies	que tu sois
qu'	il/elle/on ait	que il/elle/on soit
	plural	**plural**
que	nous ayons	que nous soyons
que	vous ayez	que vous soyez
qu'	ils/elles aient	que ils/elles soient

6-16a Verbs with irregular stems

savoir *(to know)*	**sach**	+ subjunctive endings
pouvoir) *(to be able)*	**puiss**	+ subjunctive endings
faire *(to do, to make)*	**fass**	+ subjunctive endings
pleuvoir *(to rain)*	qu'il pleuve	
falloir *(to be necessary)*	qu'il faille	
valoir *(to be worth)*	qu'il vaille	

6-16b Verbs with two different irregular stems

✔ One ending is used for **je, tu, il, elle** and **ils, elles**, while the second is used for **nous** and **vous**.

aller	→	**aill**	+ subjunctive endings
(to go)	→	**all**	+ subjunctive endings

singular	**plural**
que j'**aill** e	que nous **all** ions
que tu **aill** es	que vous **all** iez
qu' il/elle/on **aill** e	qu'ils/elles **aill** aient

boire *(to drink)*	→ →	boi buv	**croire** *(to believe)*	→ →	croi croy	**devoir** *(to have to, to owe)*	→ →	doiv dev
prendre *(to take)*	→ →	prenn pren	**recevoir** *(to receive)*	→ →	reçoiv recev	**tenir** *(hold)*	→ →	tienn ten
valoir *(to be worth)*	→ →	vaill val	**venir** *(to come)*	→ →	vienn ven	**voir** *(to see)*	→ →	voi voy
vouloir *(to want)*	→ →	veuill voul						

6-17 Uses of the subjunctive

6-17a The subjunctive after verbs expressing a wish, a necessity, or an obligation

aimer *to like*	avoir besoin de *to need*	conseiller *to advise*	demander *to ask*
défendre, interdire *to forbid*	désirer *to desire*	empêcher *to prevent*	exiger *demand*
préférer *to prefer*	recommander *to recommend*	souhaiter *to wish*	suggérer *to suggest*
vouloir *to want*			

Je suggère que tu **te lèves** tôt.
I suggest that you get up early.

J'exige que vous **soyez** ici à l'heure!
I demand that you be here on time!

Je souhaite que vous **réussissiez** à l'examen.
I hope you succeed on the test.

✔ When the verbs **conseiller, défendre, empêcher, interdire, ordonner, permettre, recommander,** and **suggérer** are preceded by an indirect object pronoun or followed by à + **an indirect object,** use **de + infinitive,** instead of **que** plus **subjunctive.**

Il nous a interdit **d'écrire** mais il nous a permis **de lire** le journal.
He forbade us to write, but he let us read the newspaper.

Les parents ordonnent à leurs enfants **d'aller** au lit.
The parents order their children to go to bed.

✔ Use the subjunctive if the subject in the main and in the subordinate clause is different. If there is no subject change, use the infinitive.

Je voudrais que **vous** finissiez votre roman.
I would like you to finish your novel.

Il voudrait **finir** son roman.
He would like to finish his novel.

6-17b The subjunctive after expressions of joy, regret, sorrow, fear, and surprise

être (heureux/content/ravi. . .) *to be (happy/happy/delighted. . .)*	**que** *that*

être heureux que *to be happy*	être content que *to be happy*	être ravi que *to be delighted*	être désolé que *to be sorry*
être malheureux que *to be unhappy*	être triste que *to be sad*	être furieux que *to be furious*	être étonné que *to be astonished*
être surpris que *to be surprised*	être fier que *to be proud*	déplorer que *to deplore*	aimer que, amer mieux que *to prefer*
avoir peur que *to be afraid*	craindre que *to be fear*	regretter que *to be sorry*	s'attendre à ce que *to expect*

Avoir peur and **craindre** require **ne** before the subjunctive verb.

Je crains **qu'il ne puisse** venir.
I am afraid he cannot come.

This **ne** is called the *expletive ne* and can be translated as a single negative part. This is considered a writing style used for emphasis. In this case it isn't negative and is not translated.

J'ai peur **que ce ne soit** vrai.
I am afraid this is true.

On regrette qu'elle **parte**.
We are sorry she is leaving.

Je suis fier que ma fille **soit** si généreuse.
I am proud that my daughter is so generous.

✔ Use the subjunctive if the subject in the main and in the subordinate clause is different. If there is no subject change, use the infinitive.

Il est content que **sa mère** soit revenue.
He is happy that his mother came back.

Je suis contente de **pouvoir** partir.
I am happy to be able to leave.

✔ The subjunctive is used when the actions in both clauses take place simultaneously or when the action in the subordinate clause takes place after the action or idea in the main clause.

✔ The verb of the main clause can be in the present, past, future, or conditional.

Je suis content que tu sois ici. *(now)*
I am happy you are here.

J'étais content que tu sois ici. *(yesterday)*
I was happy you were here.

Je serai content que tu sois ici. *(tomorrow)*
I will be happy you'll be here. (I will be happy when you're here.)

Je serais content que tu sois ici. *(one day)*
I would be happy that you were here. (I would be happy if you were here.)

6-17c The subjunctive after conjunctions and impersonal expressions

concession

bien que, quoique *even though, although*	quoi que *whatever*	où que *wherever*
que...ou non *whether...or not*	quel que *whatever, whichever*	qui que *whoever*

Jean aime chanter bien **qu'il n'ait** pas une belle voix.
Jean likes to sing even though he doesn't have a beautiful voice.

J'irai avec toi **où que** tu **ailles**.
I will go with you wherever you go.

purpose

afin que *in order that*	pour que *so that*

Je te prêterai mon livre pour que tu **puisses** lire l'histoire.
I will lend you my book so you can read the story.

fear

de crainte que *for fear that*	de peur que *for fear that*

J'ai peur de lui dire la vérité **de crainte qu'il ne réagisse** violemment.
I am afraid to tell him the truth for fear he will react violently.

restriction

à moins que *unless*	à condition que *on condition that*	pourvu que *provided that*	avant que *before*
jusqu'à ce que *until*	en attendant que *while, until*	sans que *without*	

Je ne serai pas tranquille **jusqu'à ce que** tu **finisses** tes devoirs.
I will not rest easy until you finish your homework.

Je t'attendrai **pourvu que** tu ne **sois** pas en retard.
I will wait for you provided that you are not late.

6-17d The subjunctive after impersonal expressions

il est bon que *it is good that*	il est désirable que *it is desirable that*	il est dommage que *it is a pity that*
il est douteux que *it is doubtful that*	il est étonnant que *it is astonishing that*	il faut que *it is necessary that*
il est important que *it is important that*	il est nécessaire que *it is necessary that*	il est obligatoire que *it is obligatory that*
il est préférable que *it is preferable that*	il est temps que *it is time that*	il est utile, inutile que *it is useful, useless that*
il vaut mieux que *it is better that*		

Il vaut mieux **que vous étudiiez** la leçon.
It is better that you study the lesson.

✔ If the subject of the sentence is neither expressed nor implied, the expressions shown in the box above are followed by an infinitive.

Il vaut mieux **étudier**.
It is better to study.

6-17e The subjunctive with verbs and expressions of doubt

douter que *to doubt that*	nier que *to deny that*	ne pas penser que *not to think that*
ne pas être certain que *not to be certain that*	ne pas être clair que *not to be clear that*	ne pas être sûr que *not to be sure that*

✔ The verbs **croire, trouver, penser, être sûr, être certain, avoir l'impression, imaginer, espérer** among others, are followed by the subjunctive when used in the negative, which implies doubt.

Je **ne** crois **pas** qu'il **vienne**.
I don't believe he'll come.

Je **ne** suis **pas** sûr qu'il **vienne**.
I am not sure he'll come.

Je **ne** pense **pas** qu'il **vienne**.
I don't think that he'll come.

but

Je suis sûr (certain) qu'il **viendra**.   Je pense qu'il **viendra**.
I am sure he'll come.   *I think that he'll come.*

Je crois qu'il **viendra**.
I believe he'll come.

✔ After a question introduced by **est-ce-que** or when intonation implies doubt, use the indicative, not the subjunctive.

Est-ce que tu crois qu'elle **viendra** demain?
Do you think she'll come tomorrow?

Vous pensez que son oeuvre **est** intéressante?
Do you think his work is interesting?

✔ However if inversion is used, employ the subjunctive.

Croyez-vous qu'elle **puisse** nous aider?
Do you think she would be able to help us?

6-17f Use of the subjunctive when the existence of the antecedent is doubtful

The subjunctive in adjective clauses.

When a clause is used as an adjective to describe a person, place or thing, the verb can be in the indicative or subjunctive.

✔ Use the subjunctive if the antecedent is indefinite, nonexistent, or hypothetical.

Ya-t-il parmi vous quelqu'un qui **sache** danser?
Is there anyone among you who knows how to dance?

Nous cherchons quelqu'un qui **puisse** nous aider.
We are looking for someone could help us.

✔ When the antecedent is negative, the subjunctive is used after the words **rien, personne, aucun**(e), **pas un**(e), **seul**(e), **pas de,** and **ne... que.**

Il n'y a personne qui **connaisse** M. Martin?
Is there no one who knows Mr. Martin?

Nous ne trouvons aucun livre qui **parle** des Mayas.
We can't find any books on the Mayas.

✔ Use the indicative if the antecedent is definite, specific, or known to exist.

Je cherche la jeune fille qui **sait** danser.
I am looking for the girl that knows how to dance.

Je connais un restaurant qui **sert** un excellent coq au vin.
I know a restaurant that serves an excellent coq au vin.

✔ The following verbs can be followed either by the indicative or the subjunctive, depending on whether or not they express a simple statement, a judgement, or an opinion.

admettre	comprendre	dire
to admit	*to understand*	*to say*
écrire	entendre	être d'avis
to write	*to hear*	*to feel, to think*
expliquer	prétendre	se plaindre
to explain	*to claim*	*to complain*
téléphoner		
to telephone		

François **admet** qu'il **a eu** tort.
François admits he was wrong.

François n'**admet** pas qu'on lui **dise** qu'il a tort.
François doesn't admit that someone says he's wrong.

Le professeur **a dit** que l'examen **serait** difficile.
The professor said the test would be difficult.

Cela **explique** que les étudiants **n'aient pas réussi**.
That explains why the students didn't succeed.

✔ Idiomatic expressions with **à + ce que** and the subjunctive

consentir	être disposé	être habitué
to consent to	*to be ready*	*to be used to*
jusqu'	s'attendre	s'engager
until	*to expect*	*to undertake, to promise*
s'opposer	tenir	veiller
to be opposed to	*to insist*	*to see to it, to make sure that*

…à ce que

Il s'attend **à ce qu'**elle **revienne**.
He expects her to come back.

6-18 The past subjunctive *is formed with the present subjunctive of the auxiliary verb* **avoir** *or* **être** *plus the* **past participle** *of the verb (p. 81).*

✔ The past subjunctive is used when the action or idea expressed in the subordinate clause took place or needed to take place before the action or the idea in the main clause.

✔ The verb in the main clause can be in present, past, future, or conditional.

Je **suis** contente que tu **aies réussi** à l'examen.
I'm glad that you did well on the test.

Il **aurait fallu** qu'il **soit parti** avant trois heures.
It would have been necessary for him to leave before three.

Bien qu'il **ait** déjà **été** en Espagne plusieurs fois il **voudrait** y revenir avec nous.
Although he had already been to Spain several times, he would like to go back there with us.

✔ The past subjunctive is used to express that something must be completed before specific deadlines.

Il faut que vous **soyez arrivé** avant midi.
It is necessary that you arrive before noon.

Je voudrais qu'il **soit parti** avant la fin de la semaine.
I would like him to leave before the end of the week.

✔ Use the subjunctive with a superlative, or the following expressions: **le seul** *(the only)*, **l'unique** *(the unique)*, **le premier** *(the first)*, **le dernier** *(the last)*. You can use **jamais** for emphasis.

C'est **le meilleur** film que j'aie **jamais** vu.
This is the best movie I've ever seen.

6-19 The imperfect and the pluperfect subjunctive are literary tenses.

6-19a **The imperfect subjunctive** is formed by dropping the ending of the passé simple and adding the imperfect subjunctive endings.

chanter *(to sing)*			finir *(to finish)*			perdre *(to lose)*		
subjunctive	stem +	ending	subjunctive	stem +	ending	subjunctive	stem +	ending
		singular			**singular**			**singular**
qu' je	chant	-asse	que je	fin	-isse	que je	perd	-usse
qu' tu	chant	-asses	que tu	fin	-isses	que tu	perd	-usses
qu'il/elle/on	chant	-ât	qu'il/elle/on	fin	-ît	qu'il/elle/on	perd	-ût
		plural			**plural**			**plural**
qu' nous	chant	-assions	que nous	fin	-issions	que nous	perd	-ussions
qu' vous	chant	-assiez	que vous	fin	-issiez	que vous	perd	-ussiez
qi'ils/elles	chant	-assent	qu'ils/elles	fin	-issent	qu'ils/elles	perd	-ussent

"Il leur importait peu **que je souffrisse** à cause d'eux."
"They were indifferent that I suffered because of them."

François Mauriac, Noeud de vipères

✔ Verbs ending in **-cer** and **-ger** have spelling changes in all the forms.

commen**cer**	que je commen**ç**asse
man**ger**	qu'ils mang**e**assent

✔ The imperfect is used to show simultaneous actions or that an action occurred after the action of the main verb.

Il fût désolé qu'ils **refusassent** de le faire.
He was very disappointed they refused to do it.

Le chef d'orchestre ordonna que les musiciens **répétassent** le mouvement trois fois de suite.
The conductor ordered the musicians to repeat the movement three times in a row.

6-19b The pluperfect subjunctive is formed with the imperfect subjunctive of the auxiliary verb **avoir** or **être** and **the past participle** (p. 81).

payer
(to pay)

singular	**plural**
que j'eusse payé	que nous eussions payé
que tu eusses payé	que vous eussiez payé
qu'il/elle/on eût payé	qu'ils/elles eussent payé

aller
(to go)

singular	**plural**
que je fusse allé(e)	que nous fussions allé(e)s
que tu fusses allé(e)	que vous fussiez allé(e)(s)
qu'il/elle/on fût allé(e)	qu'ils/elles fussent allé(e)s

✔ In a subordinate clause, the pluperfect subjunctive is used to express anteriority in reference to a previous action.

Gustavo craignait que ses camarades ne l'**eussent trahi**.
Gustavo feared that his comrades had betrayed him.

"La vue de la petite madeleine ne m'avait rien rappelé avant que je n'y **eusse goûté** ... "
"The sight of the small sponge-cake didn't remind me of anything until I had tasted it..."

Marcel Proust, Du côté de chez Swann

✔ Used with the conditional, the pluperfect subjunctive expresses correlation.

S'il lui **eût parlé**, elle aurait compris qu'il l'aimait.
If he had spoken to her, she would have understood that he loved her.

CHART 12   SUBJUNCTIVE OR INDICATIVE?

USE SUBJUNCTIVE	← SUBJUNCTIVE OR INDICATIVE? →	USE INDICATIVE
✔	← **Doubt:** douter, être possible, **ne pas** croire, **ne pas** penser	
	but être probable, espérer, croire, penser imply certainty →	✔
✔	← **Requests:** prier, supplier, demander... **que**	
	but prier, supplier, demander... **de** → **infinitive**	
✔	← **Willingness:** aimer, désirer, insister à, préférer, permettre, vouloir, exiger, ordonner, défendre, empêcher, recommander, suggérer, conseiller... **que**	
	but ordonner, défendre, interdire, empêcher, recommander, suggérer, permettre, conseiller... **de** → **infinitive**	
✔	← **Emotion:** être...heureux, ...ravi, ...désolé, ...malheureux, ...triste, ...furieux, ...étonné, ...surpris, craindre, regretter **que**	
	but if there is no change in subject, use **de + infinitive**	
✔	← **Impersonal expressions:** il est...bon, ...désirable, ...dommage, ...douteux, étonnant, ...important, ...temps, ...nécessaire, ...obligatoire, ...utile (inutile), ...préférable, il faut (vaut) mieux **que**...	
✔	*but* when the subject is neither expressed nor implied, use **de + infinitive** with impersonal expressions that express a certainty. C'est...certain, ...vrai, ...sûr que →	✔
✔	← **Pourvu que:** before the verb to express doubt or uncertainty	
✔	← **Adverb clauses:** relating an event or action that is indefinite or uncertain, pour que, afin que, sans que, à moins que, à condition que, avant que, pourvu que, de peur que, bien que, quoique, jusqu'à ce que	
	After: malgré que, lorsque, pendant que, après que, jusqu'à ce que, dès que to introduce forthcoming events, hypothetical actions or something that has not yet occurred, or to refer to an action that has happened, is happening, or habitually happens. →	✔
✔	← **Adjective clauses:** If the antecedent is indefinite, nonexistent, hypothetical, or negative	
	but if the antecedent is definite, specific, or known to exist →	✔
✔	**After:** admettre, comprendre, dire, écrire, entendre, expliquer, se plaindre, prétendre, téléphoner, être d'avis...	
✔	← **Appreciation:** judgement or opinion statement →	✔

CHART 13   PATTERNS OF CONJUGATION FOR REGULAR -ER, -IR, AND -RE VERBS

	verb ending	infinitive minus	+	infinitive minus	+	nous form of the present indicative minus	+
			PRESENT	PASSÉ COMPOSÉ Present tense of **avoir** or **être** + past participle		IMPERFECT	
je	**er**	-er	-e	-er	-é	-ons	-ais
tu			-es		-é		-ais
il/elle/on			-e		-é		-ait
nous			-ons		-é		-ions
vous			-ez		-é		-iez
ils/elles			-ent		-é		-aient
je	**ir**	- ir	-is	-ir	-i	-ons	-ais
tu			-is		-i		-ais
il/elle/on			-it		-i		-ait
nous			-issons		-i		-ions
vous			-issez		-i		-iez
ils/elles			-issent		-i		-aient
je	**re**	-re	-s	-re	-u	-ons	-ais
tu			-s		-u		-ais
il/elle/on			-		-u		-ait
nous			-ons		-u		-ions
vous			-ez		-u		-iez
ils/elles			-ent		-u		-aient

CHART 13   PATTERNS OF CONJUGATION, CONTINUED

	verb ending	FUTURE infinitive	+	CONDITIONAL infinitive	+	SUBJUNCTIVE **ils** form of the present indicative minus -ent	+
je	-er	infinitive	-ai	infinitive	-ais	-ent	-e
tu			-as		-ais		-es
il/on/elle			-a		-ait		-e
nous			-ons		-ions		-ions
vous			-ez		-iez		-iez
il/elles			-ont		-aient		-ent
je	-ir	infinitive	-ai	infinitive	-ais	-ent	-e
tu			-as		-ais		-es
il/ elle/on			-a		-ait		-e
nous			-ons		-ions		-ions
vous			-ez		-iez		-iez
ils/elles			-ont		-aient		-ent
je	-re	infinitive minus -e	-ai	infinitive	-ais	-ent	-e
tu			-as		-ais		-es
il/elle			-a		-ait		-e
nous			-ons		-ions		-ions
vous			-ez		-iez		-iez
ils/elles			-ont		-aient		-ent

6-20 The imperative *is a verb tense that expresses commands, requests, or directions.*

✔ The **tu, vous,** and **nous** forms of the present indicative without the subject pronoun are used to form the imperative.

✔ Irregular verbs in the imperative appear below.

être (*to be*)	**avoir** (*to have*)	**savoir** (*to know*)	**vouloir** (*to want*)
sois	aie	sache	veuillez
soyons	ayons	sachons	
soyez	ayez	sachez	

Veuillez vous asseoir.
Please, have a seat.

✔ In the negative forms of the imperative, **ne,** or **n'** in front of a vowel or mute *h*, precedes the verb and **pas** follows it.

N'ayez **pas** peur.
Don't be afraid.

✔ Verbs with an irregular stem in the present are irregular in the imperative.

✔ Verbs ending in -**er** plus **aller, offrir, souffrir, ouvrir, couvrir, découvrir** and **recouvrir,** drop the -**s** of the **tu** form in the imperative except in front of **y** and **en.**

Va te coucher! Vas-y!
Go to bed! Go!

✔ In the affirmative form of the imperative, object pronouns follow the verb and are attached by a hyphen. The object pronouns -**me** and -**te** become **moi** and **toi.**

					moi
					toi
			le		lui
verb	+	hyphen	+	la	+	nous
			les		vous
					leur

Donnez-**le** moi!
Give it to me!

✔ In a negative command, object and reflexive pronouns precede the verb.

	①	②	③			
	me	le	lui			
	te					
ne	+	la	+	+	verb	pas
	vous					
	nous	les	leur			

You can use 1 & 2 and 2 & 3 together.

① ② Ne **me le** donnez pas!
Don't give it to me!

② ③ Ne **le lui** donne pas!
Don't give it to him!

① ② Ne **te les** lave pas!

(Ne te lave les mains!)
Don't wash them!

✔ The pronouns **y** and **en** directly precede the verb.

Ne m'**en** parle pas!
Don't talk to me about that!

N'**y** pense plus!
Don't think about it anymore!

CHART 14   COMPARISON OF VERB TENSES IN FRENCH AND ENGLISH

FRANÇAIS: PARLER	ENGLISH: TO TALK, TO SPEAK
Présent je parle	**Present** *I speak*
Présent progressif je suis en train de + infinitif je suis en train de parler	**Present progressive** present of **to be** + **-ing form** *I'm speaking*
Passé composé présent **être** ou **avoir** + participe passé j'ai parlé	**Present perfect** **have/has** + past participle *I have spoken*
Passé simple je parlai	**Past or preterite** *I spoke*
Passé progressif J'étais en train de + infinitif J'étais en train de parler	**Past progressive** **was, were** + **-ing form** *I was speaking*
Passé antérieur passé simple **d'avoir** or **être** + participe passé J'eus parlé	**Past perfect** **had** + past participle *I had spoken*
Imparfait Je parlais	**Imperfect** *I used to speak, I was speaking*
Plus-que-parfait imparfait **d'avoir** or **être** + participe passé j'avais parlé	**Pluperfect** **the past perfect** had + past participle *I had spoken*
Futur Je parlerai	**Future** *I will (shall) speak, I will be speaking*
Futur immédiat (proche) présent **d'aller** + infinitive Je vais parler	**Near Future** **to be going** + **infinitive** *I'm going to speak*
Futur antérieur futur **d'avoir** ou **être** + participe passé j'aurai parlé	**Future Perfect** **will (shall) have** + past participle *I will have spoken*
Futur progressif j'aurai été + en train de... J'aurai été en train de parler	**Future Progressive** **will/shall have been** + present participle *I will have been speaking*

CHART 14   COMPARISON OF VERB TENSES, CONTINUED

FRANÇAIS: PARLER	ENGLISH: TO TALK, TO SPEAK
Conditionnel présent infinitif + terminaisons je parlerais	**Present Conditional** **would +** base form of verb *I would speak*
Conditionnel passé conditionnel présent **d'avoir** ou **être** + participe passé j'aurais parlé	**Perfect Conditional** *would + have +* past participle *I would have spoken*
Subjonctif présent radical de la 3ème personne plurielle de l'indicatif présent + terminaisons que je parle	**Present Subjunctive** **present minus -s of the third-person** **base form of the verb** *that I speak*
L'imparfait du Subjonctif passé simple de l'indicatif + terminaisons que je parlasse	**Imperfect Subjunctive** **past tense indicative** *that I spoke*
Le passé du Subjonctif présent du subjonctif **d'avoir** ou **être** +participe passé que j'aie parlé	Present Perfect Subjunctive **present perfect indicative** *that I have spoken*
Le plus-que-parfait du subjonctif imparfait du subjonctif d'avoir ou être +participe passé que j'eusse parlé	Pluperfect or **Past Perfect Subjunctive** **past perfect indicative** *that I had spoken*
The imperative is formed with the present indicative verb forms of the second-person singular, the second-person plural, and the first-person plural. Verbs in which the second-person singular ends in **-es** eliminate the final **s,** except when the imperative is followed by the pronouns **en** or **y.**	**Imperative** infinitive minus **to**
Parle! Parlez! Parlons! Ne parle pas! Ne…pas!	*Speak!* *Don't speak!*

6-21 Idiomatic expressions with verbs

6-21a Idiomatic expressions with **être** are used to express conditions or feelings.

✔ To modify these expressions, use the adverb **très**, but never use **beaucoup**.

être + an adjective

Je suis fatigué(e)	*I am tired*
heureux(euse)	*happy*
triste	*sad*
malade	*sick*
ennuyé(e)	*bored*
occupé(e)	*busy*
préoccupé(e)	*worried*
énervé(e)	*nervous*
content(e)	*happy*
prêt(e)	*ready*
fou/folle	*crazy*
sûr(e)	*sure*
vivant(e)	*alive*
mort(e)	*dead*

6-21b Common expressions with **être**

| **être** d'accord | *to agree with* |

Être en train de + infinitive indicate an action in progress

Je suis en train	de manger.	*I'm eating.*
	...de jouer.	*I'm playing.*
	...de étudier.	*I'm studying.*

être à l'heure	*to be on time*
en retard	*late*
en avance	*early*

| Quelle heure est-il? | Il est une heure. |
| *What time is it?* | *It is one o'clock.* |

6-21c Idiomatic expressions with **avoir**

✔ **avoir + a noun**

J'ai + faim	*I am hungry*
soif	*thirsty*
froid	*cold*
chaud	*hot*
sommeil	*sleepy*
peur	*afraid*
de la chance	*lucky*
raison	*right*
tort	*wrong*
. . . ans	*. . . years old*
honte	*ashamed*

6-21d Common expressions with **avoir**

avoir	besoin de	*to need*
	. . . envie de	*to feel like*
	. . . l'habitude de	*to be used to*
	. . . l'intention de	*to have the intention*
	. . . l'âge de	*to have the age of*

6-21e Idiomatic expressions with **faire**

✔ **faire** in expressions of time and weather

Il fait beau.	*The weather is fine.*
Il fait mauvais.	*The weather is bad*
Il fait chaud.	*It is hot*
Il fait frais.	*It is cool*
Il fait froid.	*It is cold*
Il fait doux.	*It is mild*
Il fait du vent.	*It is windy*
Il fait du soleil.	*It is sunny*
Il fait jour.	*It is daylight*
Il fait nuit.	*It is dark*
Il fait sec.	*It is dry*
Il fait humide.	*It is humid*
Il fait bon.	*It is nice*
Il fait de l'orage.	*It is stormy*
Il se fait tard.	*It is getting late.*

✔ **Other** common expressions with **faire**

Ça fait bien!	*That's good.*
Ça fait mal!	*That hurts!*
Ça fait du bien.	*It does one good.*
Ça fait du mal.	*It does one harm.*
Ça ne fait rien.	*It doesn't matter.*
C'est bien fait!	*That will teach you!*

6-22 Mener/Porter

✔ **Mener** and its compounds **amener, ramener, emmener,** and **remmener** are used for persons, animals, or objects able to move by themselves.

✔ **Porter** and its compounds **apporter, rapporter, emporter,** and **remporter** are generally used for objects you need to move.

✔ Mener means *to lead.*

✔ Porter means *to carry.*

✔ Amener means *to bring* someone to another place.

Mes parents m'**amenaient** chez mon cousin pour les vacances, puis ils rentraient à Paris.
My parents used to bring me to my cousin's house for vacations, then they returned to Paris.

✔ **Ramener** means *to bring back.*

Amenez votre copine à la fête mais souvenez-vous, si vous prenez plus de deux verres, demandez à un ami de vous **ramener** chez vous.
Bring your friend to the party; but remember, if you drink more than two glasses of beer, ask a friend to bring you back home.

✔ **Emmener** means *to take someone along.*

Mes parents aimaient nous **emmener** avec eux en Italie.
My parents liked to take us with them to Italy.

Pierre, **emmenez**-moi dîner à La tour d'argent ce soir.
Pierre, take me to dinner at La tour d'argent tonight.

✔ **Remmener** means *to take back.*

Amenez l'enfant à l'école, puis **remmenez-le** chez lui.
Bring the child to school, then take him back home.

✔ **Apporter** means *to bring.*

✔ **Rapporter** means *to bring back.*

✔ **Emporter** means *to take something along*.

✔ **Remporter** means *to take back*.

Apportez vos livres à la classe, mais n'oubliez pas de les **remporter** à la fin du cours.
Bring your books, but don't forget to take them with you at the end of class.

6-23 Savoir/Connaître

savoir

singular	plural
je sais	nous savons
tu sais	vous savez
il/elle/on sait	ils/elles savent

Savoir means to know facts, numbers, or other specific information thoroughly.

Je sais qui est l'assassin.
I know who the murderer is.

✔ **Savoir,** when followed by an infinitive, means *to know how to do something*.

Je sais conduire.
I know how to drive.

✔ **Savoir** may be used with or without a direct object.

Je sais la leçon par coeur.   Je sais que tu sais.
I know the lesson by heart.   *I know that you know.*

✔ Use **savoir** to ask for information.

Savez-vous où se trouve la bibliothèque?
Do you know where the library is?

connaître

singular	plural
je connais	nous connaissons
tu connais	vous connaissez
il/elle/on connaît	ils/elles connaissent

Connaître means to know a person, be familiar or acquainted with things, places, or situations.

Je connais l'assassin, monsieur le juge. C'est mon mari.
I know the murderer, your honor. It's my husband.

✔ **Connaître** must be followed by a direct object.

Je connais Paris aussi bien que Barcelone.
I know Paris as well as Barcelona.

✔ Connaître can not be followed by a clause beginning with **que**.

Connaissez-vous l'oeuvre de Rimbaud?
Do you know Rimbaud's work?

6-24 Savoir/Pouvoir

Note also the distinction between **savoir** and **pouvoir**.

pouvoir

singular	**plural**
je peux	nous pouvons
tu peux	vous pouvez
il/elle/on peut	ils/elles peuvent

✔ **Savoir** plus an **infinitive** means *to know how to do something.*

✔ **Pouvoir** plus an **infinitive** means *to be able to do something.*

✔ If the verb indicates mental ability, **savoir** is used.

Savez-vous lire?
Do you know how to read?

✔ If the verb expresses physical ability, **pouvoir** is used.

Pouvez-vous courir?   Non, je ne peux pas. Ma jambe est cassée.
Can you run?   *No, I can not; my leg is broken.*

CHAPTER 7

Prepositions

Prepositions are unchanging connecting words placed before a noun to indicate the relation of the noun to a verb, an adjective, or another noun.

7-1 Prepositions of place

✔ Prepositions of place situate things and people in space.

à *in, at, to*	chez *at the house (place) of*	contre *against*	en *in, at, into*
dans *in, within*	hors de *outside, out of*	devant *in front of, before*	derrière *behind*
sous *underneath, below*	sur *on, upon*	près de/loin de *close to/far from*	à droite *on the right*
à gauche *on the left*	en haut de *over, above*	en bas de *under*	en face de *across from, facing*
à côté de *beside, next to*	de l'autre côté de *on the other side of*	le long de *along*	au milieu de *in the middle of*
entre *between*	parmi *among*	d'entre *among*	autour de *around*

✔ **Parmi** denotes more than two people or objects. It is used in front of a plural noun, or in front of a noun referring to a group.

Elle était **parmi** les invités.
She was among the guests.

Elle était **parmi** la foule.
She was among the crowd.

✔ **Entre** is used when you have only two people or objects.

Il était **entre** les deux filles.
He was between the two girls.

✔ **D'entre** is used in front of a stressed pronoun.

Dix **d'entre** eux ont passé l'examen.
Ten of them took the test.

✔ **Dans** is used with a place.

Il est dans le salon.	...dans l'armoir.	...dans la chambre.
He is in the the living room.	*...in the closet.*	*...in the bedroom.*

7-2 Prepositions of time

✔ Use prepositions of time to indicate events in time.

après	avant	dès	depuis
after	*before*	*from... on*	*since*
pendant	environ	au début de	en/à la fin de
during	*about*	*at the beginning of*	*at the end of*
au milieu de	au moment de	entre	
in the middle of	*at the time of*	*between*	

✔ Use **pour** *(for)* and a time expression to indicate a period of time to be spent.

Elle ira à Paris **pour** deux mois.
She will go to Paris for two months.

✔ Use **dans** and a time expression to indicate how much time will elapse before something begins.

Dans un mois il sera célèbre.
In a month he'll be famous.

7-3 The preposition *à*

✔ Use **à** to indicate movement toward a place or final destination.

Demain nous irons à New York.	L'autoroute arrive jusqu'à Paris.
Tomorrow we will go to New York.	*The road leads to Paris.*

✔ Use **à** after the verbs **être, habiter,** and **vivre** to indicate location without the idea of movement.

Il est à la maison.	Il habite (à) Paris.
He is at home.	*He lives in Paris.*

Note: the **à** is often dropped after **habiter.**

✔ Use **à** to indicate the place where an action or event takes place.

La pièce se joue **au** Théâtre de la Ville.
The play is showing at the Théâtre de la Ville.

✔ Á is used before a noun to express length, distance, or content.

Le prochain village est à 10 kilomètres d'ici.
The next town is ten miles from here.

✔ Á is used with modes of transportation that involve being exposed to the elements rather than in an enclosed space such as a car or train.

à cheval   à vélo   à moto
by horse   *by bike*   *by motorcycle*

✔ Use à between two nouns or a noun and an infinitive to express the use of an object.

Il faut que j'achète une machine à laver, une machine à coudre et un fer à repaser.
I must buy a washing machine, a sewing machine, and an iron.

✔ Use à after the verbs **être** and **appartenir** to indicate possession.

Cette chemise est à mon frère.   Cette voiture appartient à mon père.
This shirt is my brother's.   *This car belongs to my father.*

✔ Á is used to introduce indirect objects.

J'ai téléphoné à mon père et Pierre a écrit à ses parents.
I called my father and Pierre wrote to his parents.

7-3a   Verbs followed by the preposition à and an **infinitive**

s'amuser	apprendre	arriver	chercher	continuer
to have fun	*to learn*	*to arrive*	*to look for*	*to continue*
commencer	se décider	s'habituer	hésiter	se mettre
to begin	*to decide*	*to get used to*	*to hesitate*	*to put on, to place oneself*
parvenir	penser		réussir	tenir
to succeed, attain	*to think*		*to succeed*	*to be keen on, to be determined to*

Il **continue à travailler** sur son roman.
He continues to work on his novel.

Les enfants **ont appris à lire** et à écrire très jeunes.
The children learned how to read and write when they were very young.

7-4 The preposition *en*

✔ Use **en** to indicate a definite period of time.

en juillet, **en** été, **en** 1789
in July, in the summer, in 1789

✔ **En** is used to indicate the amount of time necessary to complete an action.

Il a fini son devoir **en** dix minutes.
He finished his homework in ten minutes.

✔ Use **en** with a noun to indicate several modes of transportation.

en voiture	**en** train	**en** bus
by car	*by train*	*by bus*

The exception is **par avion**.

une lettre **par avion**	*but*	Je voyage souvent **en avion**.
an air mail letter		*I often travel by plane.*

✔ Use **en** to tell what things are made of.

La chaise est **en** bois.	Il m'a offert une bague **en** or.
The chair is made of wood.	*He gave me a golden ring.*

✔ **En** is used to show direction or location with feminine countries or countries that start with a vowel or a muted **h**.

Je téléphone **en** France.	Il voyage **en** Italie.
I am calling in France.	*He is travelling in Italy.*

7-5 The preposition *de*

✔ **De** is used to indicate possession or belonging.

Le livre **de** Jean est magnifique.	La porte **de** ma maison n'ouvre pas.
Jean's book is magnificent.	*The door of my house doesn't open.*

✔ Use **de** to indicate a starting point or place of origin with verbs like **aller, arriver, s'éloigner, partir, sortir, venir, revenir,** etc.

On ira **de** New York à Paris *par avion*.
We will go from New York to Paris by plane.

Je viens **de** Marseille.
I come from Marseille.

✔ **De** is used to indicate a subject or theme.

«Nosferatus» est un film d' horreur. Nous parlerons **de** l'oeuvre de Proust.
"Nosferatus" is a horror movie. *We will talk about Proust's work.*

✔ Use **de** with a noun that modifies another noun.

une agence **de** voyages une robe **de** chambre
a travel agency *a dressing gown*

✔ **De** is used with some verbs to indicate cause or reason.

rougir **de** honte mourir **de** faim tomber **de** sommeil
to blush from shame *to die of hunger* *to fall asleep*

pleurer **de** joie crier **de** joie tomber **de** fatigue
to cry from joy *to scream for joy* *to be ready to drop*

7-5a Verbs followed by the preposition *de* and an infinitive

accepter *to accept*	arrêter *to stop*	avoir besoin *to need*	avoir envie *to feel like*	avoir peur *to be afraid*
cesser *to cease, to end*	choisir *to choose*	craindre *to fear*	décider *to decide*	dépêcher *to hurry*
essayer *to try*	éviter *to avoid*	faire *to do, to make*	exprimer *to express*	finir *to finish*
oublier *to forget*	refuser *to refuse*	regretter *to regret*	tâcher *to try*	commencer *to begin*
continuer *to continue*				

J'ai envie d'aller au cinéma. Nous avons **décidé de** ne pas le **prendre** au sérieux.
I feel like going to the movies. *We decided not to take him seriously.*

7-5b à cause de *(because of)*   malgré *(in spite of, despite)*

✔ The preposition **à cause de** indicates reason and is followed by a noun or pronoun. **Malgré** indicates opposition.

Il a été reconnu au niveau national **à cause de** son travail.
Because of his work he gained national recognition.

Malgré son travail il a été licencié.
Despite his work he was fired.

Tu pourras sortir **à condition que** tu *finisses* tes devoirs.
You will be able to go out provided that you finish your homework.

Au cas où tu *changerais* d'avis, téléphone-moi.
In case you change your mind, call me.

7-6 Voici and Voilà

✔ **Voici** and **voilà** are relative prepositions used to designate a person or thing relatively near or far from the speaker.

Voici mes fleurs,	*Here are my flowers,*
voici mes rêves,	*here are my dreams,*
voici ma vie.	*here is my life.*
Voilà mes fleurs qui meurent,	*Those are my dying flowers,*
voilà mes rêves qui s'évanouissent,	*those are my vanishing dreams*
voilà ma vie qui disparaît.	*that is my life as it disappears.*

CHART 15	THE PREPOSITIONS À, EN, DANS, AND DE WITH GEOGRAPHIC NAMES		
cities	**à, de** *à, de Paris*		
countries masculine	**au, du** *au, du Portugal*	beginning in a vowel **en, d'** *en, d'Equateur*	
feminine		**en, de** *en, de France*	
masculine plural	**aux, des** *aux, des Etats-Unis*		
regions—feminine and masculine beginning with a vowel		**en, de, d'** *en, de Bretagne,* *d'Anjou*	
regions—preposition + article + masculine noun beginning with a consonant			**dans, du, de l'** *dans le, du* *Piédmont, dans,* *de l'est*
islands—without an article	**à, de** *à, de Porto Rico*		
islands—with an article		**en, de** *en, de Corse*	
states		**en, de** *en, de Californie*	**dans le, du, de l'** *dans le, du* *Michigan* *de l'Ohio*

aller	à Paris **en** France **dans** le sud	*to go to*
être	à Paris **en** France **dans** le Périgord	*to be in*
(re)venir	**de** France	*to come (back) from*

Most states in the United States are masculine because their names end in letters other than -**e.**

le Texas, **l'**Ohio, **le** Connecticut

Exceptions are **le** Maine, **la** Californie, **la** Georgie, and **la** Floride.

7-7 Pour versus Par

7-7a Pour (*for*) expresses destination for a specific person, thing, or organization.

Ces fleurs sont **pour** toi.
*These flowers are **for** you.*

✔ **Pour** can mean *in the direction of*, or *toward.*

Hier ils sont partis **pour** la France.
Yesterday they left for France.

✔ **Pour** replaces **pendant** after verbs of motion or with future actions.

J'irai à Paris **pour** deux mois.
I will go to Paris for two months.

✔ **Pour** plus an infinitive means *in order to.*

Je suis venu **pour** te dire au revoir.
I came to say goodbye.

Pour commencer, je voudrais vous parler de Molière.
To begin, I would like to talk about Molière.

✔ **Pour que** expresses a goal (*so that*).

Je vous enseigne **pour que** vous puissiez réussir.
I teach you so you can succeed.

✔ Use **pour** when considering, comparing with others, or to express an opinion.

Rien n'est difficile **pour** lui.
Nothing is difficult for him.

Pour un étranger, il parle bien le français.
For a foreigner, he speaks French well.

✔ **Pour** can mean *in the employ of.*

Il travaille **pour** le gouvernement.
He works for the government.

✔ **Pour** means *by* or *for* when expressing a deadline.

J'ai besoin du compte rendu **pour** mardi prochain, s'il vous plaît.
I need the report for next Tuesday, please.

7-7b Par is used to indicate motion through or by a place.

Il est passé **par** Paris.
He passed through Paris.

Nous sommes entrés **par** la porte principale.
We entered through the front door.

✔ **Par** is used to express the agent in the passive voice.

Ce livre a été écrit **par** un maître.
This book was written by a master.

✔ After **commencer** and **finir**, use **par** followed by an **infinitive.**

J'ai fini **par** comprendre, s'écria Juliette.
I finally understand, exclaimed Juliette.

✔ Use **par** followed by **a noun** to express frequency or amount per unit of time.

Je vais en France deux fois **par** an.
I go to France twice a year.

Je gagne cinquante dollars **par** jour.
I earn fifty dollars a day.

but

Je gagne dix dollars **de** l'heure.
I earn ten dollars an hour.

Je roulais à 90 kilomètres **à** l'heure.
I drove 90 kilometers an hour.

CHAPTER 8

Conjunctions

Conjunctions link words, sentences, or clauses; establishing relationships between them.

8-1 Coordinating conjunctions *connect two words, parts of a sentence, groups of words, or propositions.*

et	ou	mais	ni	or	ainsi/donc/en conséquence	car
and	*or*	*but*	*neither, nor*	*now, well*	*so, thus, therefore*	*because, for*

✔ Coordinating conjunctions join two elements of equal value.

✔ Use coordinating conjunctions to connect a word to another word.

les fraises **et** le chocolat
strawberries and chocolate

✔ Use coordinating conjunctions to connect a phrase to an independent phrase.

Tu peux te garer au garage **ou** devant la maison.
You can park in the garage or in front of the house.

✔ Coordinate conjunctions can connect a dependent clause to another dependent clause.

Je suis allé au théâtre **mais** je suis arrivé trop tard.
I went to the theater, but I arrived too late.

✔ Use coordinating conjunctions to connect an independent clause to another independent clause.

Il aime avoir de l'argent **mais** il hait travailler.
He likes to make money, but he hates to work.

8-2 **Conjunctions of time** *introduce previous, simultaneous, or posterior conditions.*

quand *when*	avant que *before*	après que *after*	pendant que *while*	aussitôt que* *as soon as*
dès que *as soon as*	jusqu'à ce que *until*		lorsque, quand* *when*	

*After these conjunctions, the future tense is used whenever there is a future implied.

Nous irons au cinéma **dès que** tu auras fini tes devoirs.
We'll go to the movies as soon as you've finished your homework.

8-3 **Conjunctions of purpose** *link an independent clause to a dependent clause.*

à moins que *unless*	pourvu que *provided that*	à condition que *provided that*	sans que *without*
afin que *in order that*	pour que *so that*	tant que *as long as*	au cas où *in case*

Most of these conjunctions are followed by the subjunctive, with the exception of **tant que** and **au cas où** that take the indicative or conditional.

8-4 **Subordinating or adverbial conjunctions** *link a subordinate clause to the main clause.*

après que *after*	quoique *although*	comme *as*	tant que *as long as*	dès que *as soon as*
parce que *because*	maintenant *now that*	afin que *in order that*	si *if*	ainsi que *as well as, like*
que *than*	pendant *while*	comme si *as if*	avant que *before*	depuis *since*
à moins que *unless*	jusqu'à *until*	quand *when*	car *because, for*	où *where*
bien que *although*	puisque *since*			

Nous irons à la fête **quoique** nous soyons fatigués.
We will go to the party although we are tired.

Ouvrez la porte **afin que** les invités puissent entrer.
Open the door so that the guests can come in.

Tant qu'il pourra écrire, je serai tranquille.
As long as he is able to write, I will be at peace.

S'il vous plaît, traitez-moi **comme si** j'étais votre frère, dit Caïn.
Please, treat me as if I were your brother, said Cain.

Je ne peux pas aller au théâtre **parce que** je suis malade.
I can't go to the theater because I'm sick.

8-5 Adversative conjunctions *express antithesis or opposition.*

mais	sinon*	au contraire de	cependant
but	*otherwise, if not*	*on the contrary, despite of*	*nevertheless*

*In spoken French, **autrement** or **sans ça** are used instead of **sinon**.

Au contraire de ce que tu penses il a réussi dans la vie.
Despite what you think, he suceeded in life.

Prends tes médicaments, **sinon** tu ne guériras jamais.
Take your medicine; otherwise, you will never get well.

CHAPTER 9

Accents and diacritics

✔ There are three written accent marks in French.

  accent aigu é   accent grave à, è, ù   accent circonflexe â, ê, î, ô, û

✔ The **accent aigu** is only used on the letter -e, which is then pronounced [e] instead of [ə]

  téléphone   doré   parlé   Américain   chanté

✔ When an **accent grave** is used on the letter -e, the pronunciation changes to [ɛ].

✔ The letter -è is often followed by a consonant and a mute -e.

  père   mère   célèbre ténèbres

✔ On the vowels à or ù, an accent grave is used to distinguish between homonyms.

il a	à
he has	*to, at*
ou	où
or	*where*
la	là
the	*there*

✔ The **accent circonflexe** causes the pronunciation of the vowel to be longer than it would without it.

  pâte   tête   connaît

✔ The **accent circonflexe** is also used to distinguish between homonyms.

cote	côte
rating, standing	*rib, coast*
du	dû
of, the, some	*owed, due*
sur	sûr
on	*sure*
mur	mûre
wall	*ripe*

✔ The **cédille** is placed under a **c** [ç] in front of the vowels **a, o** or **u** to soften the pronunciation to an **s**.

    ça   français   François

✔ The **tréma**, used with **ë, ï, ü,** is placed on the second of two consecutive vowels so that each vowel is pronounced separately.

    naïf   Noël   aiguë   Saül

CHAPTER 10

Stress

✔ Stress is usually placed on the last pronounced vowel of a word in French.

     chemin   journal   émotion

✔ However, a mute **e** at the end of a word, even if it is pronounced, is never stressed.*

     parle   latitude

Note: the endings -e and -**es** of polysyllables, as well as the -**ent** ending of verbs in the third-person plural, are silent.

     porte   portes   portent

CHAPTER 11

Syllabication

✔ All French words are divided into as many syllables as there are vowel sounds.

11-1 How to divide words into syllables

1. When a consonant and a vowel appear together, divide after the vowel.

consonant vowel ÷

pe ti te   gé né ral   mi di

ch, ph are considered single consonants

che mi se   Chi li   té lé **pho** ne   **pho** to

2. When two consonants appear together, divide between the consonants.

consonant ÷ consonant

ac teur   ar ti cle   gros se   pro gram me

However, never divide a **consonant** followed by an **l** or **r**.

pr ÷   **gl ÷**   **bl ÷**
après   ai **gle**   in vi si **ble**

3. When three consonants appear together, divide before the last consonant.

consonant consonant ÷ consonant

ins ti tu tion

However, if an **l** or **r** follows two consonants, divide after the first consonant.

com **pli** ment   com **pren** dre

4. When four consonants appear together, divide in the middle.

consonant consonant ÷ consonant consonant

cons trui re   ins truc teur

✔ The following are single syllables formed by the combination of two or three vowels.

ai	lait	**au**	au to	**eau**	beau
ei	veine	**eu**	pleu reur	**eui**	é cu reuil
oei	oeil	**oeu**	oeuvre	**oi**	voi là
oie	oie	**ou**	cou rir	**oui**	Louis
ui	cuis son				

11-2 The division of words at the end of a line

✔ The following syllabic division is usually used.

cons-cience   cons-pirer

Never divide a word so that a silent syllable is sent to the next line. The division must leave at least two letters at the end of a line.

✘ publi-que   mélan-ge
✔ pu-blique   mé-lange

Never divide *before* or *after* an **x** or a **y** between two vowels.

✘ infle-xible   deu-xième   vo-yeur
✘ inflex-ible   deux-ième   voy-eur

✔ **However,** the division between **x** and **y** is possible whenever they are followed by a consonant.

✔ tex-ture   pay-sage   pay-san

✔ Sets of initials are never divided.

✘ O.-N.U
✔ O.N.U.   O.E.A.   O.T.A.N.   P.T.T.

✔ Do not divide titles from the names that follow.

✘ Mme.-Pernaud   M.-Proust
✔ Mme. Pernaud   M. Proust

✔ Do not divide a compound name of letters and numbers.

✘ Paul -VI   Léon -XIII   Vème-République
✔ Paul VI   Léon XIII   Vème République

✔ Do not divide dates.

✘ le 14 -juillet   le 14 juillet -1789
✔ le 14 juillet   le 14 juillet 1789

CHAPTER 12

Liaison

✔ Liaison occurs when the usually-silent final consonant of a word is pronounced when followed by a word beginning with a vowel, or mute h.

The letters **s, x, t, d, r, p, g, f** and **n** are usually not pronounced, but with liaison they are pronounced as follows.

s x z	[z]	les amis, aux armes, allez-y
t, d	[t]	petit enfant, grand enfant
r	[r]	le premier arrivé
p	[p]	trop aimable
g	[g]	long attente
f	[v]	neuf ans
n	[n]	bon ami

✔ The endings **-rd** and **-rt** form the liaison with the **r** and not with the **d** or the **t**.

regard étonné   (regarétonné)

Mandatory liaisons

Liaison is necessary in the following circumstances.

✔ Liaison occurs between the definite and indefinite articles, the demonstrative and possessive adjectives, interrogative and exclamation words and **a noun**.

les amis   un arbre   aux armes   ces enfants

✔ Between the definite and indefinite articles, the demonstrative and possessive adjectives, interrogative and exclamation words and **an adjective** or **a noun**.

mes anciens amis

✔ Liaison occurs between one or two pronouns and **a verb**.

Ils en ont.   Allez-y!

✔ Liaison occurs after **an adverb,** or **a monosyllabic preposition,** and after **après**.

bien aimable   très amical   après avoir parlé

✔ Liaison occurs after **quand** et **dont.**

> quand‿on publiera mon livre...

Forbidden Liaisons

✘ The liaison never occurs after a singular noun.

✘ The liaison never occurs after **et.**

✘ The liaison never occurs in front of an aspirate **h.**

✘ The liaison never occurs in front of **onze** and **oui.**

✘ The liaison never occurs in plural compound nouns.

> salles à manger

✘ The liaison never occurs in front of [j] or [w] in foreign nouns.

✘ Do not use the liaison between **ils, elles,** or **on** and **an infinitive** or **past participle.**

> Vont-ils arriver?

✘ The liasion is not used after **comment, quand,** and **combien.**

> The exception is Comment‿allez-vous?

INDEX OF VERBS

Regular, Stem-Changing, Irregular, and Reflexive Verbs

Note: Numbers indicate where each verb is located in the verb index.

INDEX OF VERBS (Continued)

Regular, Stem-Changing, Irregular, and Reflexive Verbs

REGULAR VERBS

1. Regular -er verbs: *chanter*, abandonner, abîmer, abriter, (s')absenter, absorber, abuser, accabler, accentuer, accepter, accoucher, accuser, adapter, admirer, adopter, adorer, adresser, affecter, affirmer, affoler, affronter, (s')agiter, ajouter, aider, aimer, alarmer, alerter, alimenter, améliorer, (s')amuser, (s')angoisser, animer, apaiser, apporter, apprivoiser, arrêter, arriver, assassiner, assembler, assister, attacher, attirer, avaler, avouer, bavarder, blesser, briser, bronzer, brosser, cacher, calculer, calmer, cambrioler, captiver, caresser, chercher, combiner, comparer, compenser, confirmer, conseiller, constater, conter, continuer, contrôler, couper, danser, déchirer, décider, demander, désirer, détester, donner, (s')empêcher, entrer, éviter, (s')excuser, habiter, (s')habituer, hésiter, inviter, laisser, (se) laver, monter, oublier, parler, passer, penser, préparer, présenter, proposer, quitter, remercier, refuser, rêver, souhaiter, travailler

SUBJECT	PRESENT	PASSÉ COMPOSÉ	IMPERFECT	PLUPERFECT	FUTURE	CONDITIONAL	PRESENT SUBJUNCTIVE	IMPERATIVE
je	chant e	j'ai chant é	chant ais	j'avais chant é	chanter ai	chanter ais	chant e	
tu	chant es	as chant é	chant ais	avais chant é	chanter as	chanter ais	chant es	chant e
il/elle/on	chant e	a chant é	chant ait	avait chant é	chanter a	chanter ait	chant e	
nous	chant ons	avons chant é	chant ions	avions chant é	chanter ons	chanter ions	chant ions	chant ons
vous	chant ez	avez chant é	chant iez	aviez chant é	chanter ez	chanter iez	chant iez	chant ez
ils/elles	chant ent	ont chant é	chant aient	avaient chant é	chanter ont	chanter aient	chant ent	

Infinitive: chant er
Future perfect: j'aurai chanté
Present participle: chant ant
Conditional perfect: j'aurais chanté
Past participle: chant é
Present perfect subjunctive: j'aie chanté

2. Regular -ir verbs: *finir*, applaudir, bâtir, choisir, farcir, frémir, garantir, grandir, guérir, impartir, invertir, investir, jaillir, jaunir, jouir, languir, lotir, maudire, moisir, noircir, nourrir, obéir, pâlir, polir, punir, raccourcir, ramollir, rassortir, ravir, réagir, réfléchir, réjouir, remplir, répartir, resurgir, rétablir, retentir, rétrécir, réunir, réussir, rôtir, rougir, saisir, subir, tiédir, trahir, unir, verdir, vernir, vomir, maudire* (* conjugated like finir)

SUBJECT	PRESENT	PASSÉ COMPOSÉ	IMPERFECT	PLUPERFECT	FUTURE	CONDITIONAL	PRESENT SUBJUNCTIVE	IMPERATIVE
je	fin is	j'ai fin i	finiss ais	j'avais fin i	finir ai	finir ais	fin isse	
tu	fin is	as fin i	finiss ais	avais fin i	finir as	finir ais	fin isses	fin is
il/elle/on	fin it	a fin i	finiss ait	avait fin i	finir a	finir ait	fin isse	
nous	fin issons	avons fin i	finiss ions	avions fin i	finir ons	finir ions	fin issions	fin issons
vous	fin issez	avez fin i	finiss iez	aviez fin i	finir ez	finir iez	fin issiez	fin issez
ils/elles	fin issent	ont fin i	finiss aient	avaient fin i	finir ont	finir aient	fin issent	

Infinitive: fin ir
Future perfect: j'aurai fini
Present participle: finiss ant
Conditional perfect: j'aurais fini
Past participle: fin i
Present perfect subjunctive: j'aie fini

3. Regular -re verbs: *perdre*, attendre, confondre, défendre, dépendre, descendre, entendre, étendre, fondre, interrompre, mordre, pendre, perdre, pondre, prétendre, remordre, rendre, répandre, repondre, répondre, sous-entendre, tendre, tordre, vendre; rompre*, corrompre*, and interrompre* (* add a **t** in the third-person singular form of the present indicative: il rompt)

SUBJECT	PRESENT	PASSÉ COMPOSÉ	IMPERFECT	PLUPERFECT	FUTURE	CONDITIONAL	PRESENT SUBJUNCTIVE	IMPERATIVE
je	perd s	j'ai perd u	perd ais	j'avais perd u	perdr ai	perdr ais	perd e	
tu	perd s	as perd u	perd ais	avais perd u	perdr as	perdr ais	perd es	perd s
il/elle/on	perd	a perd u	perd ait	avait perd u	perdr a	perdr ait	perd e	
nous	perd ons	avons perd u	perd ions	avions perd u	perdr ons	perdr ions	perd ions	perd ons
vous	perd ez	avez perd u	perd iez	aviez perd u	perdr ez	perdr iez	perd iez	perd ez
ils/elles	perd ent	ont perd u	perd aient	avaient perd u	perdr ont	perdr aient	perd ent	

Infinitive: perd re
Future perfect: j'aurai perdu
Present participle: perd ant
Conditional perfect: j'aurais perdu
Past participle: perd u
Present perfect subjunctive: j'aie perdu

4. -er verbs: spelling changes (eler → ell) (eter → ett) *appeler*, jeter

SUBJECT	PRESENT	PASSÉ COMPOSÉ	IMPERFECT	PLUPERFECT	FUTURE	CONDITIONAL	PRESENT SUBJUNCTIVE	IMPERATIVE
j'	appell e	ai appel é	appel ais	avais appel é	appeller ai	appeller ais	appell e	
tu	appell es	as appel é	appel ais	avais appel é	appeller as	appeller ais	appell es	appell e
il/elle/on	appell e	a appel é	appel ait	avait appel é	appeller a	appeller ait	appell e	
nous	appel ons	avons appel é	appel ions	avions appel é	appeller ons	appeller ions	appel ions	appel ons
vous	appel ez	avez appel é	appel iez	aviez appel é	appeller ez	appeller iez	appel iez	appel ez
ils/elles	appell ent	ont appel é	appel aient	avaient appel é	appeller ont	appeller aient	appell ent	

Infinitive: appel er
Future perfect: j'aurai appelé
Past participle: appel é
Present perfect subjunctive: j'aie appelé
Present participle: appel ant
Conditional perfect: j'aurais appelé

5. -er verbs: spelling changes (y → i) *payer*, balayer, bégayer, broyer, dérayer, effrayer, égayer, employer, ennuyer, essayer, flamboyer, foudroyer, larmoyer, nettoyer, noyer, rayer, reployer, tutoyer, vouvoyer

SUBJECT	PRESENT	PASSÉ COMPOSÉ	IMPERFECT	PLUPERFECT	FUTURE	CONDITIONAL	PRESENT SUBJUNCTIVE	IMPERATIVE
je	pai e	ai pay é	pay ais	avais pa y é	paier ai	paier ais	pai e	
tu	pai es	as pay é	pay ais	avais pay é	paier as	paier ais	pai es	pai e
il/elle/on	pai e	a pay é	pay ait	avait pay é	paier a	paier ait	pai e	
nous	pay ons	avons pay é	pay ions	avions pay é	paier ons	paier ions	pay ions	pay ons
vous	pay ez	avez pay é	pay iez	aviez pay é	paier ez	paier iez	pay iez	pay ez
ils/elles	pai ent	ont pay é	pay aient	avaient pay é	paier ont	paier aient	pai ent	

Infinitive: pay er
Future perfect: j'aurai payé
Past participle: pay é
Present perfect subjunctive: j'aie payé
Present participle: pay ant
Conditional perfect: j'aurais payé

6. -er verbs: spelling changes (y → i) *envoyer*, renvoyer Irregular in the future & the conditional

SUBJECT	PRESENT	PASSÉ COMPOSÉ	IMPERFECT	PLUPERFECT	FUTURE	CONDITIONAL	PRESENT SUBJUNCTIVE	IMPERATIVE
j'	envoi e	ai envoy é	envoy ais	avais envoy é	**enverrai**	enverrais	envoi e	
tu	envoie s	as envoy é	envoy ais	avais envoy é	enverras	enverrais	envoi es	envoi e
il/elle/on	envoi e	a envoy é	envoy ait	avait envoy é	enverra	enverrait	envoi e	
nous	envoy ons	avons envoy é	envoy ions	avions envoy é	enverrons	enverrions	envoy ions	envoy ons
vous	envoy ez	avez envoy é	envoy iez	aviez envoy é	enverrez	enverriez	envoy iez	envoy ez
ils/elles	envoi ient	ont envoy é	envoy aient	avaient envoy é	enverront	enverraient	envoi ent	

Infinitive: envoy er
Future perfect: j'aurai envoyé
Past participle: envoy é
Present perfect subjunctive: j'aie envoyé
Present participle: envoy ant
Conditional perfect: j'aurais envoyé

7. -er verbs: spelling changes (c → ç) *commencer*, agacer, agencer, amorcer, annoncer, avancer, balancer, bercer, concurrencer, dédicacer, défoncer, dénoncer, déplacer, désamorcer, distancer, divorcer, effacer, (s')efforcer, enfoncer, énoncer, épicer, exercer, (se) fiancer, forcer, glacer, grincer, influencer, menacer, percer, pincer, placer, prononcer, recommencer, remplacer, renoncer, retracer, rincer, tracer, transpercer

SUBJECT	PRESENT	PASSÉ COMPOSÉ	IMPERFECT	PLUPERFECT	FUTURE	CONDITIONAL	PRESENT SUBJUNCTIVE	IMPERATIVE
je	commenc e	j'ai commenc é	commenç ais	j'avais commenc é	commencer ai	commencer ais	commenc e	
tu	commenc es	as commenc é	commenç ais	avais commenc é	commencer as	commencer ais	commenc es	commenc e
il/elle/on	commenc e	a commenc é	commenç ait	avait commenc é	commencer a	commencer ait	commenc e	
nous	commenç ons	avons commenc é	commenc ions	avions commenc é	commencer ons	commencer ions	commenc ions	commenç ons
vous	commenc ez	avez commenc é	commenc iez	aviez commenc é	commencer ez	commencer iez	commenc iez	commenc ez
ils/elles	commenc ent	ont commenc é	commenç aient	avaient commenc é	commencer ont	commencer aient	commenc ent	

Infinitive: commenc er
Future perfect: j'aurai commencé
Past participle: commenc é
Present perfect subjunctive: j'aie commencé
Present participle: commenç ant
Conditional perfect: j'aurais commencé

8. -er verbs: spelling changes (g → ge) *manger*, adjuger, allonger, arranger, bouger, changer, charger, converger, corriger, décourager, dégager, déménager, déranger, désavantager, dévisager, diriger, diverger, égorger, élonger, émerger, encourager, enrager, envisager, éponger, exiger, figer, forger, héberger, infliger, (s')insurger, juger, loger, longer, mélanger, mitiger, nager, neiger, obliger, outrager, partager, piger, plonger, préjuger, présager, prolonger, propager, rager, ranger, ravager, rédiger, ronger, songer, soulager, submerger, surcharger, venger, voltiger, voyager

SUBJECT	PRESENT	PASSÉ COMPOSÉ	IMPERFECT	PLUPERFECT	FUTURE	CONDITIONAL	PRESENT SUBJUNCTIVE	IMPERATIVE
je	mang e	j'ai mang é	mange ais	j'avais mang é	manger ai	manger ais	mang e	
tu	mang es	as mang é	mange ais	avais mang é	manger as	manger ais	mang es	mang e
il/elle/on	mang e	a mang é	mange ait	avait mang é	manger a	manger ait	mang e	
nous	mange ons	avons mang é	mangi ons	avions mang é	manger ons	manger ions	mang ions	mange ons
vous	mang ez	avez mang é	mangi ez	aviez mang é	manger ez	manger iez	mang iez	mang ez
ils/elles	mang ent	ont mang é	mange aient	avaient mang é	manger ont	manger aient	mang ent	

Infinitive: mang er
Future perfect: j'aurai mangé
Present participle: mange ant
Conditional perfect: j'aurais mangé
Past participle: mang é
Present perfect subjunctive: j'aie mangé

9. -er accent mark change (e → è): *acheter*, celer, congeler, déceler, dégeler, démanteler, écarteler, geler, lever, mener, modeler, peler, racheter, receler

SUBJECT	PRESENT	PASSÉ COMPOSÉ	IMPERFECT	PLUPERFECT	FUTURE	CONDITIONAL	PRESENT SUBJUNCTIVE	IMPERATIVE
j'	achèt e	ai achet é	achet ais	avais achet é	achèter ai	achèter ais	achèt e	
tu	achèt es	as achet é	achet ais	avais achet é	achèter as	achèter ais	achèt es	achèt e
il, elle	achèt e	a achet é	achet ait	avait achet é	achèter a	achèter ait	achèt e	
nous	achet ons	avons achet é	achet ions	avions achet é	achèter ons	achèter ions	achet ions	achet ons
vous	achet ez	avez achet é	achet iez	aviez achet é	achèt erez	achèter iez	achet iez	achet ez
ils/elles	achèt ent	ont achet é	achet aient	avaient achet é	achèt eront	achèter aient	achèt ent	

Infinitive: achet er
Future perfect: j'aurai acheté
Present participle: achet ant
Conditional perfect: j'aurais acheté
Past participle: achet é
Present perfect subjunctive: j'aie acheté

10. -er accent mark change (é → è) verbs ending in: éder (*céder*), ébrer (célébrer), écer (macérer), écher (lécher), écrer (exécrer), égler (régler), égner (im-prégner), égrer (intégrer), éguer (déléguer), éler (accélérer), émer (blasphémer), éner (aliéner), érer (préférer), éser (aléser), éter (répéter), étrer (chronométrer)

SUBJECT	PRESENT	PASSÉ COMPOSÉ	IMPERFECT	PLUPERFECT	FUTURE	CONDITIONAL	PRESENT SUBJUNCTIVE	IMPERATIVE
je	céd e	j'ai céd é	céd ais	avais céd é	céder ai	céder ais	céd e	
tu	céd es	as céd é	céd ais	avais céd é	céder as	céder ais	céd es	céd e
il/elle/on	céd e	a céd é	céd ait	avait céd é	céder a	céder ait	céd e	
nous	céd ons	avons céd é	céd ions	avions céd é	céder ons	céder ions	céd ions	céd ons
vous	céd ez	avez céd é	céd iez	aviez céd é	céder ez	céder iez	céd iez	céd ez
ils/elles	céd ent	ont céd é	céd aient	avaient céd é	céder ont	céder aient	céd ent	

Infinitive: céd er
Future perfect: j'aurai cédé
Present participle: céd ant
Conditional perfect: j'aurais cédé
Past participle: céd é
Present perfect subjunctive: j'aie cédé

11. -oir changing verbs: (c → ç) *recevoir*, apercevoir, concevoir, décevoir, percevoir

SUBJECT	PRESENT	PASSÉ COMPOSÉ	IMPERFECT	PLUPERFECT	FUTURE	CONDITIONAL	PRESENT SUBJUNCTIVE	IMPERATIVE
je	re çois	j'ai re çu	recev ais	avais re çu	recevr ai	recevr ais	reçoiv e	
tu	re çois	as re çu	recev ais	avais re çu	recevr as	recevr ais	reçoiv es	re çois
il/elle/on	re çoit	a re çu	recev ait	avait re çu	recevr a	recevr ait	reçoiv e	
nous	re cevons	avons re çu	recev ions	avions re çu	recevr ons	recevr ions	recev ions	re cevons
vous	re cevez	avez re çu	recev iez	aviez re çu	recevr ez	recevr iez	recev iez	re cevez
ils/elles	re çoivent	ont re çu	recev aient	avaient re çu	recevr ont	recevr aient	reçoiv ent	

Infinitive: recev oir
Future perfect: j'aurai reçu
Present participle: recev ant
Conditional perfect: j'aurais reçu
Past participle: re çu
Present perfect subjunctive: j'aie reçu

12. verbs ending in -aître: (i → î) *connaître*, apparaître, comparaître, disparaître, méconnaître, paraître, réapparaître, reconnaître

SUBJECT	PRESENT	PASSÉ COMPOSÉ	IMPERFECT	PLUPERFECT	FUTURE	CONDITIONAL	PRESENT SUBJUNCTIVE	IMPERATIVE
je	conn **ais**	ai conn **u**	connaiss **ais**	avais conn **u**	connaîtr **ai**	connaîtr **ais**	connaiss **e**	
tu	conn **ais**	as conn **u**	connaiss **ais**	avais conn **u**	connaîtr **as**	connaîtr **ais**	connaiss **es**	conn **ais**
il/elle/on	conn **aît**	a conn **u**	connaiss **ait**	avait conn **u**	connaîtr **a**	connaîtr **ait**	connaiss **e**	
nous	conn **aissons**	avons conn **u**	connaiss **ions**	avions conn **u**	connaîtr **ons**	connaîtr **ions**	connaiss **ions**	conn **aissons**
vous	conn **aissez**	avez conn **u**	connaiss **iez**	aviez conn **u**	connaîtr **ez**	connaîtr **iez**	connaiss **iez**	conn **aissez**
ils/elles	conn **aissent**	ont conn **u**	connaiss **aient**	avaient conn **u**	connaîtr **ont**	connaîtr **aient**	connaiss **ent**	

Infinitive: connaît **re**
Future perfect: j'aurai connu
Present participle: connaiss **ant**
Conditional perfect: j'aurais connu
Past participle: conn **u**
Present perfect subjunctive: j'aie connu

13. the irregular verbs naître, renaître

SUBJECT	PRESENT	PASSÉ COMPOSÉ	IMPERFECT	PLUPERFECT	FUTURE	CONDITIONAL	PRESENT SUBJUNCTIVE	IMPERATIVE
je	nais	suis né(e)	naissais	étais né(e)	naîtrai	naîtrais	naisse	
tu	nais	es né(e)	naissais	étais né(e)	naîtras	naîtrais	naisses	nais
il/elle/on	naît	est né(e)	naissait	était né(e)	naîtra	naîtrait	naisse	
nous	naissons	sommes né(e)s	naissions	étions né(e)s	naîtrons	naîtrions	naissions	naissons
vous	naissez	êtes né(e)s	naissiez	étiez né(e)s	naîtrez	naîtriez	naissiez	naissez
ils/elles	naissent	sont né(e)s	naissaient	étaient né(e)s	naîtront	naîtraient	naissent	

Infinitive: naît **re**
Future perfect: je serai né(e)
Present participle: naiss **ant**
Conditional perfect: je serais né(e)
Past participle: **né(e)**
Present perfect subjunctive: je sois né(e)

14. verbs ending in -re with double consonants: *mettre**, admettre, commettre, compromettre, émettre, omettre, permettre, promettre, soumettre, transmettre; (battre*, abattre, combattre, débattre)

SUBJECT	PRESENT	PASSÉ COMPOSÉ	IMPERFECT	PLUPERFECT	FUTURE	CONDITIONAL	PRESENT SUBJUNCTIVE	IMPERATIVE
je	mets	ai mis	mettais	avais mis	mettrai	mettrais	mette	
tu	mets	as mis	mettais	avais mis	mettras	mettrais	mettes	mets
il/elle/on	met	a mis	mettait	avait mis	mettra	mettrait	mette	
nous	mettons	avons mis	mettions	avions mis	mettrons	mettrions	mettions	mettons
vous	mettez	avez mis	mettiez	aviez mis	mettrez	mettriez	mettiez	mettez
ils/elles	mettent	ont mis	mettaient	avaient mis	mettront	mettraient	mettent	

Infinitive: mett **re**
Future perfect: j'aurai mis
Present participle: mett **ant**
Conditional perfect: j'aurais mis
Past participle: **mis**
Present perfect subjunctive: j'aie mis

*Form the stem of the singular forms by dropping the -re ending plus one consonant.

15. acquérir

SUBJECT	PRESENT	PASSÉ COMPOSÉ	IMPERFECT	PLUPERFECT	FUTURE	CONDITIONAL	PRESENT SUBJUNCTIVE	IMPERATIVE
j'	acquiers	ai acquis	acquérais	avais acquis	acquerrai	acquerrais	acquière	
tu	acquiers	as acquis	acquérais	avais acquis	acquerras	acquerrais	acquières	acquiers
il/elle/on	acquiert	a acquis	acquérait	avait acquis	acquerra	acquerrait	acquière	
nous	acquérons	avons acquis	acquérions	avions acquis	acquerrons	acquerrions	acquérions	acquérons
vous	acquérez	avez acquis	acquériez	aviez acquis	acquerrez	acquerriez	acquériez	acquérez
ils/elles	acquièrent	ont acquis	acquéraient	avaient acquis	acquerront	acquerraient	acquièrent	

Infinitive: acquér **ir**
Future perfect: j'aurai acquis
Present participle: acquér **ant**
Conditional perfect: j'aurais acquis
Past participle: **acquis**
Present perfect subjunctive: j'aie acquis

16. aller

SUBJECT	PRESENT	PASSÉ COMPOSÉ	IMPERFECT	PLUPERFECT	FUTURE	CONDITIONAL	PRESENT SUBJUNCTIVE	IMPERATIVE
je	vais	suis allé(e)	j'allais	j'étais allé(e)	j'irai	j'irais	j'aille	
tu	vas	es allé(e)	allais	étais allé(e)	iras	irais	ailles	va
il/elle/on	va	est allé(e)	allait	était allé(e)	ira	irait	aille	
nous	allons	sommes allé(e)s	allions	étions allé(e)s	irons	irions	allions	allons
vous	allez	êtes allé(e)s	alliez	étiez allé(e)s	irez	iriez	alliez	allez
ils/elles	vont	sont allé(e)s	allaient	étaient allé(e)s	iront	iraient	aillent	

Infinitive: **aller**   Present participle: **allant**   Past participle: **allé(e)**
Future perfect: je serai allé(e)   Conditional perfect: je serais allé(e)   Present perfect subjunctive: je sois allé(e)

17. avoir

SUBJECT	PRESENT	PASSÉ COMPOSÉ	IMPERFECT	PLUPERFECT	FUTURE	CONDITIONAL	PRESENT SUBJUNCTIVE	IMPERATIVE
j'	ai	ai eu	avais	avais eu	aurai	aurais	aie	
tu	as	as eu	avais	avais eu	auras	aurais	aies	aie
il/elle/on	a	a eu	avait	avait eu	aura	aurait	ait	
nous	avons	avons eu	avions	avions eu	aurons	aurions	ayons	ayons
vous	avez	avez eu	aviez	aviez eu	aurez	auriez	ayez	ayez
ils/elles	ont	ont eu	avaient	avaient eu	auront	auraient	aient	

Infinitive: **avoir**   Present participle: **ayant**   Past participle: **eu**
Future perfect: j'aurai eu   Conditional perfect: j'aurais eu   Present perfect subjunctive: j'aie eu

18. boire

SUBJECT	PRESENT	PASSÉ COMPOSÉ	IMPERFECT	PLUPERFECT	FUTURE	CONDITIONAL	PRESENT SUBJUNCTIVE	IMPERATIVE
je	bois	j'ai bu	buvais	j'avais bu	boirai	boirais	boive	
tu	bois	as bu	buvais	avais bu	boiras	boirais	boives	bois
il/elle/on	boit	a bu	buvait	avait bu	boira	boirait	boive	
nous	buvons	avons bu	buvions	avions bu	boirons	boirions	buvions	buvons
vous	buvez	avez bu	buviez	aviez bu	boirez	boiriez	buviez	buvez
ils/elles	boivent	ont bu	buvaient	avaient bu	boiront	boiraient	boivent	

Infinitive: **boire**   Present participle: **buvant**   Past participle: **bu**
Future perfect: j'aurai bu   Conditional perfect: j'aurais bu   Present perfect subjunctive: j'aie bu

19. conclure

SUBJECT	PRESENT	PASSÉ COMPOSÉ	IMPERFECT	PLUPERFECT	FUTURE	CONDITIONAL	PRESENT SUBJUNCTIVE	IMPERATIVE
je	conclus	j'ai conclu	concluais	j'avais conclu	conclurai	conclurais	conclue	
tu	conclus	as conclu	concluais	avais conclu	concluras	conclurais	conclues	conclus
il/elle/on	conclut	a conclu	concluait	avait conclu	conclura	conclurait	conclue	
nous	concluons	avons conclu	concluions	avions conclu	conclurons	conclurions	concluions	concluons
vous	concluez	avez conclu	concluiez	aviez conclu	conclurez	concluriez	concluiez	concluez
ils/elles	concluent	ont conclu	concluaient	avaient conclu	concluront	concluraient	concluent	

Infinitive: **conclure**   Present participle: **concluant**   Past participle: **conclu**
Future perfect: j'aurai conclu   Conditional perfect: j'aurais conclu   Present perfect subjunctive: j'aie conclu

20. coudre

SUBJECT	PRESENT	PASSÉ COMPOSÉ	IMPERFECT	PLUPERFECT	FUTURE	CONDITIONAL	PRESENT SUBJUNCTIVE	IMPERATIVE
je	couds	j'ai cousu	cousais	j'avais cousu	coudrai	coudrais	couse	
tu	couds	as cousu	cousais	avais cousu	coudras	coudrais	couses	couds
il/elle/on	coud	a cousu	cousait	avait cousu	coudra	coudrait	couse	
nous	cousons	avons cousu	cousions	avions cousu	coudrons	coudrions	cousions	cousons
vous	cousez	avez cousu	cousiez	aviez cousu	coudrez	coudriez	cousiez	cousez
ils/elles	cousent	ont cousu	cousaient	avaient cousu	coudront	coudraient	cousent	

Infinitive: **coudre**
Future perfect: **j'aurai cousu**
Present participle: **cousant**
Conditional perfect: **j'aurais cousu**
Past participle: **cousu**
Present perfect subjunctive: **j'aie cousu**

21. coûter

PRESENT	PASSÉ COMPOSÉ	IMPERFECT	PLUPERFECT	FUTURE	CONDITIONAL	PRESENT SUBJUNCTIVE
il coûte	il a coûté	il coûtait	il avait coûté	il coûtera	il coûterait	il coûte
ils coûtent	ils ont coûté	ils coûtaient	ils avaient coûté	ils coûteront	ils coûteraient	ils coûtent

Infinitive: **coûter**
Future perfect: **il aura coûté**
Present participle: **coûtant**
Conditional perfect: **il aurait coûté**
Past participle: **coûté**
Present perfect subjunctive: **il ait coûté**

22. craindre

SUBJECT	PRESENT	PASSÉ COMPOSÉ	IMPERFECT	PLUPERFECT	FUTURE	CONDITIONAL	PRESENT SUBJUNCTIVE	IMPERATIVE
je	crains	ai craint	craignais	avais craint	craindrai	craindrais	craigne	
tu	crains	as craint	craignais	avais craint	craindras	craindrais	craignes	crains
il/elle/on	craint	a craint	craignait	avait craint	craindra	craindrait	craigne	
nous	craignons	avons craint	craignions	avions craint	craindrons	craindrions	craignions	craignons
vous	craignez	avez craint	craigniez	aviez craint	craindrez	craindriez	craigniez	craignez
ils/elles	craignent	ont craint	craignaient	avaient craint	craindront	craindraient	craignent	

Infinitive: **craindre**
Future perfect: **j'aurai craint**
Present participle: **craignant**
Conditional perfect: **j'aurais craint**
Past participle: **craint**
Present perfect subjunctive: **j'aie craint**

23. croire

SUBJECT	PRESENT	PASSÉ COMPOSÉ	IMPERFECT	PLUPERFECT	FUTURE	CONDITIONAL	PRESENT SUBJUNCTIVE	IMPERATIVE
je	crois	j'ai cru	croyais	j'avais cru	croirai	croirais	croie	
tu	crois	as cru	croyais	avais cru	croiras	croirais	croies	crois
il/elle/on	croit	a cru	croyait	avait cru	croira	croirait	croie	
nous	croyons	avons cru	croyions	avions cru	croirons	croirions	croyions	croyons
vous	croyez	avez cru	croyiez	aviez cru	croirez	croiriez	croyiez	croyez
ils/elles	croient	ont cru	croyaient	avaient cru	croiront	croiraient	croient	

Infinitive: **croire**
Future perfect: **j'aurai cru**
Present participle: **croyant**
Conditional perfect: **j'aurais cru**
Past participle: **cru**
Present perfect subjunctive: **j'aie cru**

24. cueillir, *accueillir, recueillir*

SUBJECT	PRESENT	PASSÉ COMPOSÉ	IMPERFECT	PLUPERFECT	FUTURE	CONDITIONAL	PRESENT SUBJUNCTIVE	IMPERATIVE
je	cueille	j'ai cueilli	cueillais	j'avais cueilli	cueillerai	cueillerais	cueille	
tu	cueilles	as cueilli	cueillais	avais cueilli	cueilleras	cueillerais	cueilles	cueille
il/elle/on	cueille	a cueilli	cueillait	avait cueilli	cueillera	cueillerait	cueille	
nous	cueillons	avons cueilli	cueillions	avions cueilli	cueillerons	cueillerions	cueillions	cueillons
vous	cueillez	avez cueilli	cueilliez	aviez cueilli	cueillerez	cueilleriez	cueilliez	cueillez
ils/elles	cueillent	ont cueilli	cueillaient	avaient cueilli	cueilleront	cueilleraient	cueillent	

Infinitive: **cueillir**   Present participle: **cueillant**   Past participle: **cueilli**
Future perfect: j'aurai cueilli   **Conditional perfect:** j'aurais cueilli   **Present perfect subjunctive:** j'aie cueilli

25. courir, *concourir, discourir, parcourir, recourir, secourir*

SUBJECT	PRESENT	PASSÉ COMPOSÉ	IMPERFECT	PLUPERFECT	FUTURE	CONDITIONAL	PRESENT SUBJUNCTIVE	IMPERATIVE
je	cours	j'ai couru	courais	j'avais couru	courrai	courrais	coure	
tu	cours	as couru	courais	avais couru	courras	courrais	coures	cours
il/elle/on	court	a couru	courait	avait couru	courra	courrait	coure	
nous	courons	avons couru	courions	avions couru	courrons	courrions	courions	courons
vous	courez	avez couru	couriez	aviez couru	courrez	courriez	couriez	courez
ils/elles	courent	ont couru	couraient	avaient couru	courront	courraient	courent	

Infinitive: **courir**   Present participle: **courant**   Past participle: **couru**
Future perfect: j'aurai couru   **Conditional perfect:** j'aurais couru   **Present perfect subjunctive:** j'aie couru

26. cuire, *conduire, construire, déduire, détruire, enduire, introduire, instruire, nuire, produire, reconstruire, reproduire, séduire, traduire,*

SUBJECT	PRESENT	PASSÉ COMPOSÉ	IMPERFECT	PLUPERFECT	FUTURE	CONDITIONAL	PRESENT SUBJUNCTIVE	IMPERATIVE
je	cuis	j'ai cuit	cuisais	j'avais cuit	cuirai	cuirais	cuise	
tu	cuis	as cuit	cuisais	avais cuit	cuiras	cuirais	cuises	cuis
il/elle/on	cuit	a cuit	cuisait	avait cuit	cuira	cuirait	cuise	
nous	cuisons	avons cuit	cuisions	avions cuit	cuirons	cuirions	cuisions	cuisons
vous	cuisez	avez cuit	cuisiez	aviez cuit	cuirez	cuiriez	cuisiez	cuisez
ils/elles	cuisent	ont cuit	cuisaient	avaient cuit	cuiront	cuiraient	cuisent	

Infinitive: **cuire**   Present participle: **cuisant**   Past participle: **cuit**
Future perfect: j'aurai cuit   **Conditional perfect:** j'aurais cuit   **Present perfect subjunctive:** j'aie cuit

27. devoir

SUBJECT	PRESENT	PASSÉ COMPOSÉ	IMPERFECT	PLUPERFECT	FUTURE	CONDITIONAL	PRESENT SUBJUNCTIVE	IMPERATIVE
je	dois	j'ai dû	devais	j'avais dû	devrai	devrais	doive	
tu	dois	as dû	devais	avais dû	devras	devrais	doives	dois
il/elle/on	doit	a dû	devait	avait dû	devra	devrait	doive	
nous	devons	avons dû	devions	avions dû	devrons	devrions	devions	devons
vous	devez	avez dû	deviez	aviez dû	devrez	devriez	deviez	devez
ils/elles	doivent	ont dû	devaient	avaient dû	devront	devraient	doivent	

Infinitive: **devoir**   Present participle: **devant**   Past participle: **dû**
Future perfect: j'aurai dû   **Conditional perfect:** j'aurais dû   **Present perfect subjunctive:** j'aie dû

28. dire, contredire, dédire, interdire, prédire, redire

Infinitive: **dire**
Future perfect: **j'aurai dit**

SUBJECT	PRESENT	PASSÉ COMPOSÉ	IMPERFECT	PLUPERFECT	FUTURE	CONDITIONAL	PRESENT SUBJUNCTIVE	IMPERATIVE
je	dis	j'ai dit	disais	j'avais dit	dirai	dirais	dise	
tu	dis	as dit	disais	avais dit	diras	dirais	dises	dis
il/elle/on	dit	a dit	disait	avait dit	dira	dirait	dise	
nous	disons	avons dit	disions	avions dit	dirons	dirions	disions	disons
vous	dites	avez dit	disiez	aviez dit	direz	diriez	disiez	dites
ils/elles	disent	ont dit	disaient	avaient dit	diront	diraient	disent	

Present participle: **disant**   Past participle: **dit**
Conditional perfect: **j'aurais dit**   Present perfect subjunctive: **j'aie dit**

29. écrire, circonscrire, décrire, inscrire, prescrire, proscrire, récrire, réinscrire, souscrire, transcrire

Infinitive: **écrire**
Future perfect: **j'aurai écrit**

SUBJECT	PRESENT	PASSÉ COMPOSÉ	IMPERFECT	PLUPERFECT	FUTURE	CONDITIONAL	PRESENT SUBJUNCTIVE	IMPERATIVE
je	écris	ai écrit	écrivais	avais écrit	écrirai	écrirais	écrive	
tu	écris	as écrit	écrivais	avais écrit	écriras	écrirais	écrives	écris
il/elle/on	écrit	a écrit	écrivait	avait écrit	écrira	écrirait	écrive	
nous	écrivons	avons écrit	écrivions	avions écrit	écrirons	écririons	écrivions	écrivons
vous	écrivez	avez écrit	écriviez	aviez écrit	écrirez	écririez	écriviez	écrivez
ils/elles	écrivent	ont écrit	écrivaient	avaient écrit	écriront	écriraient	écrivent	

Present participle: **écrivant**   Past participle: **écrit**
Conditional perfect: **j'aurais écrit**   Present perfect subjunctive: **j'aie écrit**

30. être

Infinitive: **être**
Future perfect: **j'aurai été**

SUBJECT	PRESENT	PASSÉ COMPOSÉ	IMPERFECT	PLUPERFECT	FUTURE	CONDITIONAL	PRESENT SUBJUNCTIVE	IMPERATIVE
je	suis	j'ai été	j'étais	j'avais été	serai	serais	sois	
tu	es	as été	étais	avais été	seras	serais	sois	sois
il/elle/on	est	a été	était	avait été	sera	serait	soit	
nous	sommes	avons été	étions	avions été	serons	serions	soyons	soyons
vous	êtes	avez été	étiez	aviez été	serez	seriez	soyez	soyez
ils/elles	sont	ont été	étaient	avaient été	seront	seraient	soient	

Present participle: **étant**   Past participle: **été**
Conditional perfect: **j'aurais été**   Present perfect subjunctive: **j'aie été**

31. faire, contrefaire, défaire, forfaire, malfaire, méfaire, refaire, satisfaire, surfaire

Infinitive: **faire**
Future perfect: **j'aurai fait**

SUBJECT	PRESENT	PASSÉ COMPOSÉ	IMPERFECT	PLUPERFECT	FUTURE	CONDITIONAL	PRESENT SUBJUNCTIVE	IMPERATIVE
je	fais	j'ai fait	faisais	j'avais fait	ferai	ferais	fasse	
tu	fais	as fait	faisais	avais fait	feras	ferais	fasses	fais
il/elle/on	fait	a fait	faisait	avait fait	fera	ferait	fasse	
nous	faisons	avons fait	faisions	avions fait	ferons	ferions	fassions	faisons
vous	faites	avez fait	faisiez	aviez fait	ferez	feriez	fassiez	faites
ils/elles	font	ont fait	faisaient	avaient fait	feront	feraient	fassent	

Present participle: **faisant**   Past participle: **fait**
Conditional perfect: **j'aurais fait**   Present perfect subjunctive: **j'aie fait**

32. joindre, rejoindre

SUBJECT	PRESENT	PASSÉ COMPOSÉ	IMPERFECT	PLUPERFECT	FUTURE	CONDITIONAL	PRESENT SUBJUNCTIVE	IMPERATIVE
je	joins	j'ai joint	joignais	j'avais joint	joindrai	joindrais	joigne	
tu	joins	as joint	joignais	avais joint	joindras	joindrais	joignes	joins
il/elle/on	joint	a joint	joignait	avait joint	joindra	joindrait	joigne	
nous	joignons	avons joint	joignions	avions joint	joindrons	joindrions	joignions	joignons
vous	joignez	avez joint	joigniez	aviez joint	joindrez	joindriez	joigniez	joignez
ils/elles	joignent	ont joint	joignaient	avaient joint	joindront	joindraient	joignent	

Infinitive: joindre
Future perfect: j'aurai joint
Present participle: joignant
Conditional perfect: j'aurais joint
Past participle: joint
Present perfect subjunctive: j'aie joint

33. lire, *élire, réélire, relire*

SUBJECT	PRESENT	PASSÉ COMPOSÉ	IMPERFECT	PLUPERFECT	FUTURE	CONDITIONAL	PRESENT SUBJUNCTIVE	IMPERATIVE
je	lis	ai lu	lisais	avais lu	lirai	lirais	lise	
tu	lis	as lu	lisais	avais lu	liras	lirais	lises	lis
il/elle/on	lit	a lu	lisait	avait lu	lira	lirait	lise	
nous	lisons	avons lu	lisions	avions lu	lirons	lirions	lisions	lisons
vous	lisez	avez lu	lisiez	aviez lu	lirez	liriez	lisiez	lisez
ils/elles	lisent	ont lu	lisaient	avaient lu	liront	liraient	lisent	

Infinitive: lire
Future perfect: j'aurai lu
Present participle: lisant
Conditional perfect: j'aurais lu
Past participle: lu
Present perfect subjunctive: j'aie lu

34. mourir

SUBJECT	PRESENT	PASSÉ COMPOSÉ	IMPERFECT	PLUPERFECT	FUTURE	CONDITIONAL	PRESENT SUBJUNCTIVE	IMPERATIVE
je	meurs	suis mort(e)	mourais	j'étais mort(e)	mourrai	mourrais	meure	
tu	meurs	es mort(e)	mourais	étais mort(e)	mourras	mourrais	meures	meurs
il/elle/on	meurt	est mort(e)	mourait	était mort(e)	mourra	mourrait	meure	
nous	mourons	sommes mort(e)s	mourions	étions mort(e)s	mourrons	mourrions	mourions	mourons
vous	mourez	êtes mort(e)s	mouriez	étiez mort(e)s	mourrez	mourriez	mouriez	mourez
ils/elles	meurent	sont mort(e)s	mouraient	étaient mort(e)s	mourront	mourraient	meurent	

Infinitive: mourir
Future perfect: je serai mort(e)
Present participle: mourant
Conditional perfect: je serais mort(e)
Past participle: mort
Present perfect subjunctive: je sois mort(e)

35. mouvoir

SUBJECT	PRESENT	PASSÉ COMPOSÉ	IMPERFECT	PLUPERFECT	FUTURE	CONDITIONAL	PRESENT SUBJUNCTIVE	IMPERATIVE
je	meus	j'ai mû	mouvais	j'avais mû	mouvrai	mouvrais	meuve	
tu	meus	as mû	mouvais	avais mû	mouvras	mouvrais	meuves	meus
il/elle/on	meut	a mû	mouvait	avait mû	mouvra	mouvrait	meuve	
nous	mouvons	avons mû	mouvions	avions mû	mouvrons	mouvrions	mouvions	mouvons
vous	mouvez	avez mû	mouviez	aviez mû	mouvrez	mouvriez	mouviez	mouvez
ils/elles	meuvent	ont mû	mouvaient	avaient mû	mouvront	mouvraient	meuvent	

Infinitive: mouvoir
Future perfect: j'aurai mû
Present participle: mouvant
Conditional perfect: j'aurais mû
Past participle: mû
Present perfect subjunctive: j'aie mû

36. ouvrir, couvrir, découvrir, entrouvrir, offrir, recouvrir, souffrir

SUBJECT	PRESENT	PASSÉ COMPOSÉ	IMPERFECT	PLUPERFECT	FUTURE	CONDITIONAL	PRESENT SUBJUNCTIVE	IMPERATIVE
j'	ouvr e	ai ouvert	ouvr ais	avais ouvert	ouvrir ai	ouvrir ais	ouvr e	
tu	ouvr es	as ouvert	ouvr ais	avais ouvert	ouvrir as	ouvrir ais	ouvr es	ouvre
il/elle/on	ouvr e	a ouvert	ouvr ait	avait ouvert	ouvrir a	ouvrir ait	ouvr e	
nous	ouvr ons	avons ouvert	ouvr ions	avions ouvert	ouvrir ons	ouvrir ions	ouvr ions	ouvrons
vous	ouvr ez	avez ouvert	ouvr iez	aviez ouvert	ouvrir ez	ouvrir iez	ouvr iez	ouvrez
ils/elles	ouvr ent	ont ouvert	ouvr aient	avaient ouvert	ouvrir ont	ouvrir aient	ouvr ent	

Infinitive: ouvrir   Present participle: **ouvrant**   Past participle: **ouvert**
Future perfect: j'aurai ouvert   **Conditional perfect:** j'aurais ouvert   **Present perfect subjunctive:** j'aie ouvert

37. partir, consentir, démentir, départir, dormir, (s')endormir*, mentir, pressentir, repartir*, se repentir*, ressentir, ressortir*, sentir, servir, sortir*

SUBJECT	PRESENT	PASSÉ COMPOSÉ	IMPERFECT	PLUPERFECT	FUTURE	CONDITIONAL	PRESENT SUBJUNCTIVE	IMPERATIVE
je	**par s**	suis part i(e)	part ais	j'étais part i(e)	partir ai	partir ais	part e	
tu	**par s**	es part i(e)	part ais	étais part i(e)	partir as	partir ais	part es	pars
il/elle/on	**par t**	est part i(e)	part ait	était part i(e)	partir a	partir ait	part e	
nous	part ons	sommes part i(e)s	part ions	étions part i(e)s	partir ons	partir ions	part ions	partons
vous	part ez	êtes part i(e)s	part iez	étiez part i(e)s	partir ez	partir iez	part iez	partez
ils/elles	part ent	sont part i(e)s	part aient	étaient part i(e)s	partir ont	partir aient	part ent	

Infinitive: partir   Present participle: **partant**   Past participle: **parti(e)**
Future perfect: je serai parti(e)   **Conditional perfect:** je serais parti(e)   **Present perfect subjunctive:** je sois parti(e)

(*Verbs conjugated with the auxiliary verb **être**)

38. prendre, *apprendre, comprendre, désapprendre, entreprendre, réapprendre, reprendre, surprendre*

SUBJECT	PRESENT	PASSÉ COMPOSÉ	IMPERFECT	PLUPERFECT	FUTURE	CONDITIONAL	PRESENT SUBJUNCTIVE	IMPERATIVE
je	prends	j'ai pris	prenais	j'avais pris	prendrai	prendrais	prenne	
tu	prends	as pris	prenais	avais pris	prendras	prendrais	prennes	prends
il/elle/on	prend	a pris	prenait	avait pris	prendra	prendrait	prenne	
nous	prenons	avons pris	prenions	avions pris	prendrons	prendrions	prenions	prenons
vous	prenez	avez pris	preniez	aviez pris	prendrez	prendriez	preniez	prenez
ils/elles	prennent	ont pris	prenaient	avaient pris	prendront	prendraient	prennent	

Infinitive: prendre   Present participle: **prenant**   Past participle: **pris**
Future perfect: j'aurai pris   **Conditional perfect:** j'aurais pris   **Present perfect subjunctive:** j'aie pris

39. pouvoir

SUBJECT	PRESENT	PASSÉ COMPOSÉ	IMPERFECT	PLUPERFECT	FUTURE	CONDITIONAL	PRESENT SUBJUNCTIVE
je	peux	j'ai pu	pouvais	j'avais pu	pourrai	pourrais	puisse
tu	peux	as pu	pouvais	avais pu	pourras	pourrais	puisses
il/elle/on	peut	a pu	pouvait	avait pu	pourra	pourrait	puisse
nous	pouvons	avons pu	pouvions	avions pu	pourrons	pourrions	puissions
vous	pouvez	avez pu	pouviez	aviez pu	pourrez	pourriez	puissiez
ils/elles	peuvent	ont pu	pouvaient	avaient pu	pourront	pourraient	puissent

Infinitive: pouvoir   Present participle: **pouvant**   Past participle: **pu**
Future perfect: j'aurai pu   **Conditional perfect:** j'aurais pu   **Present perfect subjunctive:** j'aie pu

40. rire, sourire

SUBJECT	PRESENT	PASSÉ COMPOSÉ	IMPERFECT	PLUPERFECT	FUTURE	CONDITIONAL	PRESENT SUBJUNCTIVE	IMPERATIVE
je	ris	j'ai ri	riais	j'avais ri	rirai	rirais	rie	
tu	ris	as ri	riais	avais ri	riras	rirais	ries	ris
il/elle/on	rit	a ri	riait	avait ri	rira	rirait	rie	
nous	rions	avons ri	riions	avions ri	rirons	ririons	riions	rions
vous	riez	avez ri	riiez	aviez ri	rirez	ririez	riiez	riez
ils/elles	rient	ont ri	riaient	avaient ri	riront	riraient	rient	

Infinitive: **rire**
Future perfect: **j'aurai ri**
Present participle: **riant**
Conditional perfect: **j'aurais ri**
Past participle: **ri**
Present perfect subjunctive: **j'aie ri**

41. savoir

SUBJECT	PRESENT	PASSÉ COMPOSÉ	IMPERFECT	PLUPERFECT	FUTURE	CONDITIONAL	PRESENT SUBJUNCTIVE	IMPERATIVE
je	sais	j'ai su	savais	j'avais su	saurai	saurais	sache	
tu	sais	as su	savais	avais su	sauras	saurais	saches	sache
il/elle/on	sait	a su	savait	avait su	saura	saurait	sache	
nous	savons	avons su	savions	avions su	saurons	saurions	sachions	sachons
vous	savez	avez su	saviez	aviez su	saurez	sauriez	sachiez	sachez
ils/elles	savent	ont su	savaient	avaient su	sauront	sauraient	sachent	

Infinitive: **savoir**
Future perfect: **j'aurai su**
Present participle: **sachant**
Conditional perfect: **j'aurais su**
Past participle: **su**
Present perfect subjunctive: **j'aie su**

42. suivre, (s')ensuivre, poursuivre

SUBJECT	PRESENT	PASSÉ COMPOSÉ	IMPERFECT	PLUPERFECT	FUTURE	CONDITIONAL	PRESENT SUBJUNCTIVE	IMPERATIVE
je	suis	j'ai suivi	suivais	j'avais suivi	suivrai	suivrais	suive	
tu	suis	as suivi	suivais	avais suivi	suivras	suivrais	suives	suis
il/elle/on	suit	a suivi	suivait	avait suivi	suivra	suivrait	suive	
nous	suivons	avons suivi	suivions	avions suivi	suivrons	suivrions	suivions	suivons
vous	suivez	avez suivi	suiviez	aviez suivi	suivrez	suivriez	suiviez	suivez
ils/elles	suivent	ont suivi	suivaient	avaient suivi	suivront	suivraient	suivent	

Infinitive: **suivre**
Future perfect: **j'aurai suivi**
Present participle: **suivant**
Conditional perfect: **j'aurais suivi**
Past participle: **suivi**
Present perfect subjunctive: **j'aie suivi**

43. tenir, (s')abstenir, appartenir, contenir, détenir, entretenir, obtenir, retenir, soutenir

SUBJECT	PRESENT	PASSÉ COMPOSÉ	IMPERFECT	PLUPERFECT	FUTURE	CONDITIONAL	PRESENT SUBJUNCTIVE	IMPERATIVE
je	tiens	j'ai tenu	tenais	j'avais tenu	tiendrai	tiendrais	tienne	
tu	tiens	as tenu	tenais	avais tenu	tiendras	tiendrais	tiennes	tiens
il/elle/on	tient	a tenu	tenait	avait tenu	tiendra	tiendrait	tienne	
nous	tenons	avons tenu	tenions	avions tenu	tiendrons	tiendrions	tenions	tenons
vous	tenez	avez tenu	teniez	aviez tenu	tiendrez	tiendriez	teniez	tenez
ils/elles	tiennent	ont tenu	tenaient	avaient tenu	tiendront	tiendraient	tiennent	

Infinitive: **tenir**
Future perfect: **j'aurai tenu**
Present participle: **tenant**
Conditional perfect: **j'aurais tenu**
Past participle: **tenu**
Present perfect subjunctive: **j'aie tenu**

44. vaincre

SUBJECT	PRESENT	PASSÉ COMPOSÉ	IMPERFECT	PLUPERFECT	FUTURE	CONDITIONAL	PRESENT SUBJUNCTIVE	IMPERATIVE
je	vaincs	j'ai vaincu	vainquais	j'avais vaincu	vaincrai	vaincrais	vainque	
tu	vaincs	as vaincu	vainquais	avais vaincu	vaincras	vaincrais	vainques	vaincs
il/elle/on	vainc	a vaincu	vainquait	avait vaincu	vaincra	vaincrait	vainque	
nous	vainquons	avons vaincu	vainquions	avions vaincu	vaincrons	vaincrions	vainquions	vainquons
vous	vainquez	avez vaincu	vainquiez	aviez vaincu	vaincrez	vaincriez	vainquiez	vainquez
ils/elles	vainquent	ont vaincu	vainquaient	avaient vaincu	vaincront	vaincraient	vainquent	

Infinitive: **vaincre**
Future perfect: j'aurai vaincu

Present participle: **vainquant**
Conditional perfect: j'aurais vaincu

Past participle: **vaincu**
Present perfect subjunctive: j'aie vaincu

45. valoir, équivaloir, prévaloir, revaloir

SUBJECT	PRESENT	PASSÉ COMPOSÉ	IMPERFECT	PLUPERFECT	FUTURE	CONDITIONAL	PRESENT SUBJUNCTIVE	IMPERATIVE
je	vaux	j'ai valu	valais	j'avais valu	vaudrai	vaudrais	vaille	
tu	vaux	as valu	valais	avais valu	vaudras	vaudrais	vailles	vaux
il/elle/on	vaut	a valu	valait	avait valu	vaudra	vaudrait	vaille	
nous	valons	avons valu	valions	avions valu	vaudrons	vaudrions	valions	valons
vous	valez	avez valu	valiez	aviez valu	vaudrez	vaudriez	valiez	valez
ils/elles	valent	ont valu	valaient	avaient valu	vaudront	vaudraient	vaillent	

Infinitive: **valoir**
Future perfect: j'aurai valu

Present participle: **valant**
Conditional perfect: j'aurais valu

Past participle: **valu**
Present perfect subjunctive: j'aie valu

46. venir, contrevenir, convenir, devenir, intervenir, parvenir, provenir, revenir, (se) souvenir, survenir

SUBJECT	PRESENT	PASSÉ COMPOSÉ	IMPERFECT	PLUPERFECT	FUTURE	CONDITIONAL	PRESENT SUBJUNCTIVE	IMPERATIVE
je	viens	suis venu(e)	venais	étais venue(e)	viendrai	viendrais	vienne	
tu	viens	es venu(e)	venais	étais venue(e)	viendras	viendrais	viennes	viens
il/elle/on	vient	est venu(e)	venait	était venue(e)	viendra	viendrait	vienne	
nous	venons	sommes venu(e)s	venions	étions venue(e)s	viendrons	viendrions	venions	venons
vous	venez	êtes v enu(e)s	veniez	étiez venue(e)s	viendrez	viendriez	veniez	venez
ils/elles	viennent	sont v enu(e)s	venaient	étaient venue(s)	viendront	viendraient	viennent	

Infinitive: **venir**
Future perfect: je serai venu(e)

Present participle: **venant**
Conditional perfect: je serais venu(e)

Past participle: **venu(e)**
Present perfect subjunctive: je sois venu(e)

47. vêtir

SUBJECT	PRESENT	PASSÉ COMPOSÉ	IMPERFECT	PLUPERFECT	FUTURE	CONDITIONAL	PRESENT SUBJUNCTIVE	IMPERATIVE
je	vêts	j'ai vêtu	vêtais	j'avais vêtu	vêtirai	vêtirais	vête	
tu	vêts	as vêtu	vêtais	avais vêtu	vêtiras	vêtirais	vêtes	vêts
il/elle/on	vêt	a vêtu	vêtait	avait vêtu	vêtira	vêtirait	vête	
nous	vêtons	avons vêtu	vêtions	avions vêtu	vêtirons	vêtirions	vêtions	vêtons
vous	vêtez	avez vêtu	vêtiez	aviez vêtu	vêtirez	vêtiriez	vêtiez	vêtez
ils/elles	vêtent	ont vêtu	vêtaient	avaient vêtu	vêtiront	vêtiraient	vêtent	

Infinitive: **vêtir**
Future perfect: j'aurai vêtu

Present participle: **vêtant**
Conditional perfect: j'aurais vêtu

Past participle: **vêtu**
Present perfect subjunctive: j'aie vêtu

48. vivre, revivre, survivre

SUBJECT	PRESENT	PASSÉ COMPOSÉ	IMPERFECT	PLUPERFECT	FUTURE	CONDITIONAL	PRESENT SUBJUNCTIVE	IMPERATIVE
je	vis	j'ai vécu	vivais	j'avais vécu	vivrai	vivrais	vive	
tu	vis	as vécu	vivais	avais vécu	vivras	vivrais	vives	vis
il/elle/on	vit	a vécu	vivait	avait vécu	vivra	vivrait	vive	
nous	vivons	avons vécu	vivions	avions vécu	vivrons	vivrions	vivions	vivons
vous	vivez	avez vécu	viviez	aviez vécu	vivrez	vivriez	viviez	vivez
ils/elles	vivent	ont vécu	vivaient	avaient vécu	vivront	vivraient	vivent	

Infinitive: **vivre**   Present participle: **vivant**   Past participle: **vécu**
Future perfect: j'aurai vécu   **Conditional perfect:** j'aurais vécu   **Present perfect subjunctive:** j'aie vécu

49. voir, entrevoir, prévoir, revoir

SUBJECT	PRESENT	PASSÉ COMPOSÉ	IMPERFECT	PLUPERFECT	FUTURE	CONDITIONAL	PRESENT SUBJUNCTIVE	IMPERATIVE
je	vois	j'ai vu	voyais	j'avais vu	verrai	verrais	voie	
tu	vois	as vu	voyais	avais vu	verras	verrais	voies	vois
il/elle/on	voit	a vu	voyait	avait vu	verra	verrait	voie	
nous	voyons	avons vu	voyions	avions vu	verrons	verrions	voyions	voyons
vous	voyez	avez vu	voyiez	aviez vu	verrez	verriez	voyiez	voyez
ils/elles	voient	ont vu	voyaient	avaient vu	verront	verraient	voient	

Infinitive: **voir**   Present participle: **voyant**   Past participle: **vu**
Future perfect: j'aurai vu   **Conditional perfect:** j'aurais vu   **Present perfect subjunctive:** j'aie vu

50. vouloir

SUBJECT	PRESENT	PASSÉ COMPOSÉ	IMPERFECT	PLUPERFECT	FUTURE	CONDITIONAL	PRESENT SUBJUNCTIVE	IMPERATIVE*
je	veux	j'ai voulu	voulais	j'avais voulu	voudrai	voudrais	veuille	
tu	veux	as voulu	voulais	avais voulu	voudras	voudrais	veuilles	veuille
il/elle/on	veut	a voulu	voulait	avait voulu	voudra	voudrait	veuille	
nous	voulons	avons voulu	voulions	avions voulu	voudrons	voudrions	voulions	veuillons
vous	voulez	avez voulu	vouliez	aviez voulu	voudrez	voudriez	vouliez	veuillez
ils/elles	veulent	ont voulu	voulaient	avaient voulu	voudront	voudraient	veuillent	

Infinitive: **vouloir**   Present participle: **voulant**   Past participle: **voulu**
Future perfect: j'aurai voulu   **Conditional perfect:** j'aurais voulu   **Present perfect subjunctive:** j'aie voulu

*Exception: Ne m'en VEUX pas! *(Don't hold it against me!)* Ne m'en VOULEZ pas!

Verbs preceded by the reflexive pronouns: **me, te, se, nous, vous, se** are reflexive.

verbs that are always reflexive: s'abstenir, s'emparer, s'en aller, s'enfuir, s'envoler, s'évanouir, se moquer, se repentir, se souvenir
some verbs that can be reflexive: (se) coucher, (s')endormir, (se) déshabiller, (s')habiller, (s')interroger, (se) laver, (se) lever, (se) maquiller, (se) perdre, (se) raser, (se) répondre, (se) réjouir), (se) réveiller

51. se laver to wash oneself

SUBJECT	PRESENT	PASSÉ COMPOSÉ	IMPERFECT	PLUPERFECT	FUTURE	CONDITIONAL	PRESENT SUBJUNCTIVE	IMPERATIVE
je me/m'	lav e	suis lav é(e)	lav ais	étais lav é(e)	laver ai	laver ais	lave	
tu te/t'	lav es	es lav é(e)	lav ais	étais lav é(e)	laver as	laver ais	laves	lave-toi
il/elle/on se/s'	lav e	est lav é(e)	lav ait	était lav é(e)	laver a	laver ait	lave	
nous nous	lav ons	sommes lav é(e)s	lav ions	étions lav é(e)s	laver ons	laver ions	lavions	lavons-nous
vous vous	lav ez	êtes lav é(e)s	lav iez	étiez lav é(e)s	laver ez	laver iez	laviez	lavez-vous
ils/elles se/s'	lav ent	sont lav é(e)s	lav aient	étaient lav é(e)s	laver ont	laver aient	lavent	

Infinitive: se laver · Present participle: se lavant · Past participle: lavé(e)
Future perfect: je me serai lavé(e) · Conditional perfect: je me serais lavé(e) · Present perfect subjunctive: je me sois lavé(e)

52. se réjouir to rejoice

SUBJECT	PRESENT	PASSÉ COMPOSÉ	IMPERFECT	PLUPERFECT	FUTURE	CONDITIONAL	PRESENT SUBJUNCTIVE	IMPERATIVE
je me/m'	réjou is	suis réjou i(e)	réjou issais	étais réjou i(e)	réjouir ai	réjouir ais	réjou isse	
tu te/t'	réjou is	es réjou i(e)	réjou issais	étais réjou i(e)	réjouir as	réjouir ais	réjou isses	réjouis-toi
il/elle/on se/s'	réjou it	est réjou i(e)	réjou issait	était réjou i(e)	réjouir a	réjouir ait	réjou isse	
nous nous	réjou issons	sommes réjou i(e)s	réjou issions	étions réjou i(e)s	réjouir ons	réjouir ions	réjou issions	réjouissons-nous
vous vous	réjou issez	êtes réjou i(e)s	réjou issiez	étiez réjou i(e)s	réjouir ez	réjouir iez	réjou issiez	réjouissez-vous
ils/elles se/s'	réjou issent	sont réjou i(e)s	réjou issaient	étaient réjou i(e)s	réjouir ont	réjouir aient	réjou issent	

Infinitive: se réjouir · Present participle: se réjouissant · Past participle: réjoui(e)
Future perfect: je me serai réjoui(e) · Conditional perfect: je me serais réjoui(e) · Present perfect subjunctive: je me sois réjoui(e)

53. se perdre to get lost

SUBJECT	PRESENT	PASSÉ COMPOSÉ	IMPERFECT	PLUPERFECT	FUTURE	CONDITIONAL	PRESENT SUBJUNCTIVE	IMPERATIVE
je me/m'	perd s	suis perd u(e)	perd ais	étais perd u(e)	perdr ai	perdr ais	perd e	
tu te/t'	perd s	es perd u(e)	perd ais	étais perd u(e)	perdr as	perdr ais	perd es	perds-toi
il/elle/on se/s'	perd	est perd u(e)	perd ait	était perd u(e)	perdr a	perdr ait	perd e	
nous nous	perd ons	sommes perd u(e)s	perd ions	étions perd u(e)s	perdr ons	perdr ions	perd ions	perdons-nous
vous vous	perd ez	êtes perd u(e)s	perd iez	étiez perd u(e)s	perdr ez	perdr iez	perd iez	perdez-vous
ils/elles se/s'	perd ent	sont perd u(e)s	perd aient	étaient perd u(e)s	perdr ont	perdr aient	perd ent	

Infinitive: se perdre · Present participle: se perdant · Past participle: perdu(e)
Future perfect: je me serai perdu(e) · Conditional perfect: je me serais perdu(e) · Present perfect subjunctive: je me sois perdu(e)